SCHAUM'S *Easy* OUTLINES

COLLEGE
PHYSICS

Other Books in Schaum's Easy Outlines Series include:

Schaum's Easy Outline: College Algebra
Schaum's Easy Outline: Calculus
Schaum's Easy Outline: Statistics
Schaum's Easy Outline: Programming with C++
Schaum's Easy Outline: College Chemistry
Schaum's Easy Outline: French
Schaum's Easy Outline: Spanish
Schaum's Easy Outline: German
Schaum's Easy Outline: Organic Chemistry

SCHAUM'S *Easy* OUTLINES

COLLEGE PHYSICS

BASED ON SCHAUM'S *Outline of College Physics*
BY FREDRICK J. BUECHE AND
EUGENE HECHT

ABRIDGEMENT EDITOR:
GEORGE J. HADEMENOS

SCHAUM'S OUTLINE SERIES
McGRAW-HILL

New York   San Francisco   Washington, D. C.   Auckland   Bogotá
Caracas   Lisbon   London   Madrid   Mexico City   Milan   Montreal
New Delhi   San Juan   Singapore   Sydney   Tokyo   Toronto

FREDERICK J. BUECHE, currently Distinguished Professor at Large, University of Dayton, received his Ph.D. in physics from Cornell University.

EUGENE HECHT is a member of the Physics Department of Adelphi University in New York. He has authored eight books.

GEORGE J. HADEMENOS has taught at the University of Dallas and has done research at the University of California at Los Angeles and the University of Massachusetts Medical Center. He earned a B.S.degree in Physics from Angelo State University and the M.S. and Ph.D. in Physics from the University of Texas at Dallas.

1 2 3 4 5 6 7 8 9 10 11 12 13 14 15 DOC DOC 9 0 9 8 7 6 5 4 3 2 1 0 9

ISBN 007-052711-3

Sponsoring Editor: Barbara Gilson
Production Supervisor: Tina Cameron
Editing Supervisor: Maureen B. Walker

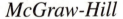

McGraw-Hill

*A Division of The **McGraw-Hill** Companies*

Contents

Chapter 1
NEWTONIAN MECHANICS

IN THIS CHAPTER:

✔ *Scalars and Vectors*
✔ *Uniformly Accelerated Motion*
✔ *Newton's Laws*
✔ *Equilibrium under the Action of Concurrent Forces*
✔ *Equilibrium of a Rigid Body under Coplanar Forces*
✔ *Work, Energy, and Power*
✔ *Impulse and Momentum*
✔ *Angular Motion in a Plane*
✔ *Rigid-Body Rotation*
✔ *Solved Problems*

Scalars and Vectors

Definitions of Scalars and Vectors

A **scalar** is a quantity that possesses only magnitude. Examples of scalar quantities are mass, length, time, distance, speed, and density.

1

A **vector** is a quantity that possesses both magnitude and direction. Examples of vector quantities are displacement, velocity, acceleration, and force. A vector quantity can be represented by an arrow drawn to scale. The length of the arrow is proportional to the magnitude of the vector quantity. The direction of the arrow represents the direction of the vector quantity.

The Components of a Vector

Before we define the components of a vector, we first must introduce the elementary relationships between trigonometric functions. The trigonometric functions are defined in relation to a right angle. For the right triangle shown in Figure 1-1, by definition

$$\sin \theta = \frac{\text{opposite}}{\text{hypotenuse}} = \frac{B}{C}$$

$$\cos \theta = \frac{\text{adjacent}}{\text{hypotenuse}} = \frac{A}{C}$$

$$\tan \theta = \frac{\text{opposite}}{\text{adjacent}} = \frac{B}{A}$$

We often use these in the forms
$$B = C \sin \theta; \quad A = C \cos \theta; \quad B = A \tan \theta$$

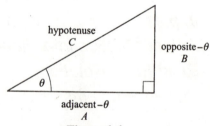

Figure 1-1

A component of a vector is its effective value in a given direction. For example, the x-component of a displacement is the displacement parallel to the x-axis caused by the given displacement. A vector in three dimensions may be considered as the resultant of its component vectors resolved along any three *mutually perpendicular* directions. Similarly, a vector in two dimensions may be resolved into two component vectors acting along any two mutually perpendicular directions. Figure 1-2 shows the vector $\vec{R}$ and its x and y vector components, $\mathbf{R}_x$, $\mathbf{R}_y$, which have magnitudes

$$\left|\vec{R}_x\right| = \left|\vec{R}\right| \cos\theta \quad \text{and} \quad \left|\vec{R}_y\right| = \left|\vec{R}\right| \sin\theta$$

or equivalently,

$$R_x = R\cos\theta \quad \text{and} \quad R_y = R\sin\theta$$

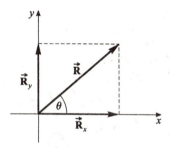

Figure 1-2

Unit Vectors

Unit vectors have a magnitude of one and are represented by a boldface symbol topped with a caret. The special unit vectors $\hat{\mathbf{i}}$, $\hat{\mathbf{j}}$, and $\hat{\mathbf{k}}$ are assigned to the x-, y-, and z-axes, respectively. A vector $3\,\hat{\mathbf{i}}$ represents a three-unit vector in the +x direction, while $-5\,\hat{\mathbf{k}}$ represents a five-unit vector in the -z direction. A vector $\vec{R}$ that has scalar x-, y-, and z-components R_x, R_y, and R_z, respectively, can be written as

$$\vec{R} = R_x\hat{\mathbf{i}} + R_y\hat{\mathbf{j}} + R_z\hat{\mathbf{k}}$$

When an object moves from one point in space to another, the **displacement** is the vector from the initial location to the final location. It is independent of the actual distance traveled.

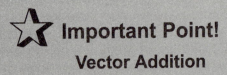

Important Point!

Vector Addition

The **resultant**, or sum, of a number of vectors of a particular type (force vectors, for example) is that single vector that would have the same effect as all the original vectors taken together.

Graphical Addition of Vectors (Polygon Method)

This method for finding the resultant $\vec{R}$ of several vectors

($\vec{A}$, $\vec{B}$, and $\vec{C}$) consists in beginning at any convenient point and drawing (to scale and in the proper directions) each vector arrow in turn. They may be taken in any order of succession:

$$\vec{A} + \vec{B} + \vec{C} = \vec{C} + \vec{A} + \vec{B} = \vec{R}$$

The tail end of each arrow is positioned at the tip end of the preceding one, as shown in Figure 1-3.

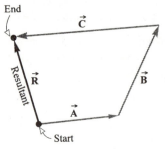

Figure 1-3

The resultant is represented by an arrow with its tail end at the starting point and its tip end at the tip of the last vector added. If $\vec{R}$ is the resultant, $R = \left|\vec{R}\right|$ is the size or **magnitude** of the resultant.

Parallelogram Method for Vector Addition

The resultant of two vectors acting at any angle may be represented by the diagonal of a parallelogram. The two vectors are drawn as the sides of the parallelogram and the resultant is its diagonal, as shown in Figure 1-4. The direction of the resultant is away from the origin of the two vectors.

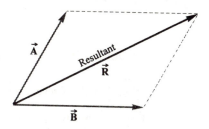

Figure 1-4

Component Method for Vector Addition

Each vector is resolved into its x-, y-, and z-components, with negatively directed components taken as negative. The scalar x-component, R_x, of the resultant $\vec{R}$ is the algebraic sum of all the scalar components. The scalar y- and z-components of the resultant are found in a similar way. With the components known, the magnitude of the resultant is given by

$$R = \sqrt{R_x^2 + R_y^2 + R_z^2}$$

In two dimensions, the angle of the resultant with the x-axis can be found from the relation

$$\tan \theta = \frac{R_y}{R_x}$$

Vector Subtraction

To subtract a vector $\vec{B}$ from a vector $\vec{A}$, reverse the direction of $\vec{B}$ and add individually to vector $\vec{A}$, that is $\vec{A} - \vec{B} = \vec{A} + (-\vec{B})$.

Uniformly Accelerated Motion

Speed is a scalar quantity. If an object takes a time interval t to travel a distance d, then

Average speed $= \dfrac{\text{total distance traveled}}{\text{time taken}}$

or

$$v_{av} = \frac{d}{t}$$

Here the distance is the total (along the path) length traveled.

Velocity is a vector quantity. If an object undergoes a vector displacement, $\vec{s}$, in a time interval, t, then

Average velocity $= \dfrac{\text{vector displacement}}{\text{time taken}}$

$$\vec{v}_{av} = \frac{\vec{s}}{t}$$

The direction of the velocity vector is the same as that of the displacement vector. The units of velocity (and speed) are those of distance divided by time, such as m/s or km/h.

Acceleration, also a vector quantity, measures the time rate-of-change of velocity:

$$\text{Average acceleration} = \frac{\text{change in velocity vector}}{\text{time taken}}$$

$$\vec{a}_{av} = \frac{\vec{v}_f - \vec{v}_i}{t}$$

where $\vec{v}_i$ is the initial velocity, $\vec{v}_f$, is the final velocity, and t is the time interval over which the change occurred. The units of acceleration are those of velocity divided by time. A typical example is (m/s)/s (or m/s^2).

Uniform Motion along a Straight Line

This represents an important situation. In this case, the *acceleration vector is constant* and lies along the line of the displacement vector, so that the directions of $\vec{v}$ and $\vec{a}$ can be specified with plus and minus signs. If we represent the displacement by s (positive if in the positive direction, and negative if in the negative direction), then the motion can be described with the five equations for uniformly accelerated motion:

$$s = v_{av} t$$

$$s = v_i t + \frac{1}{2} a t^2$$

$$v_f^2 = v_i^2 + 2as$$

$$a = \frac{v_f - v_i}{t}$$

$$v_{av} = \frac{v_f + v_i}{2}$$

Direction is important, and a positive direction must be chosen when analyzing motion along a line. Either direction may be chosen as positive. If a displacement, velocity, or acceleration is in the opposite direction, it must be taken as negative.

Instantaneous Velocity

Instantaneous velocity is the average velocity evaluated for a time interval that approaches zero. Thus, if an object undergoes a change in displacement $\Delta \vec{s}$ over a time interval Δt, then for that object the **instantaneous velocity** is

$$\vec{v} = \lim_{\Delta t \to 0} \frac{\Delta \vec{s}}{\Delta t}$$

where the notation means that the ratio $\dfrac{\Delta \vec{s}}{\Delta t}$ is to be evaluated for a time interval Δt that approaches zero.

You Need to Know

Graphical Interpretations

Graphical interpretations for motion along a straight line (the x-axis) are as follows:

• The *instantaneous velocity* of an object at a certain time is the slope of the displacement versus time graph at that time. It can be positive, negative, or zero.

• The *instantaneous acceleration* of an object at a certain time is the slope of the velocity versus time graph at that time.

• For constant-velocity motion, the x-versus-t graph is a straight line. For constant-acceleration motion, the v-versus-t graph is a straight line.

• In general (i.e., one- , two-, or three-dimensional motion), the slope at any moment of the distance-versus-time graph is the speed.

Acceleration Due to Gravity (g)

The acceleration of a body moving only under the force of gravity is g, the gravitational (or free-fall) acceleration, which is directed vertically downward. On Earth, g = 9.8 m/s^2 (i.e., 32 ft/s^2). On the Moon, the free-fall acceleration is 1.6 m/s^2.

Velocity Components

Suppose that an object moves with a velocity $\vec{v}$ at some angle θ up from the x-axis, as would initially be the case with a ball thrown into the air. That velocity then has x and y vector components of $\vec{v}_x$ and $\vec{v}_y$. The corresponding scalar components of the velocity are:

$$v_x = v \cos \theta \qquad \text{and} \qquad v_y = v \sin \theta$$

Projectile Problems

Projectile problems can be solved easily if air friction can be ignored. One simply considers the motion to consist of two independent parts: horizontal motion with a = 0 and $v_f = v_i = v_{av}$ (i.e., constant speed), and vertical motion with a = g = 9.8 m/s^2 downward.

Newton's Laws

Mass

The **mass** of an object is a measure of the inertia of the object. **Inertia** is the tendency of a body at rest to remain at rest, and of a body in motion to continue moving with unchanged velocity.

Force

Force, in general, is the agency of change. In mechanics, it is a push or a pull that changes the velocity of an object. Force is a vector quantity, having magnitude and direction. An external force is one whose source lies outside of the system being considered. The net or resultant external force acting on an object causes the object to accelerate in the direction of that force. The acceleration is proportional to the force and inversely proportional to the mass of the object. The **newton** is the SI unit of force. One newton (1 N) is that resultant force which will give a 1-kg mass an acceleration of 1 m/s². The pound is 4.45 N.

Newton's Laws

Newton's First Law: *An object at rest will remain at rest; an object in motion will continue in motion with constant velocity unless acted on by an external force.* Force is the changer of motion.

Newton's Second Law: *If the resultant or net force $\vec{F}$ acting on an object of mass m is not zero, the object accelerates in the direction of the force. The acceleration $\vec{a}$ is proportional to the force and inversely proportional to the mass of the object. With $\vec{F}$ in newtons, m in kilograms, and $\vec{a}$ in m/s², this can be written as*

$$\vec{a} = \frac{\vec{F}}{m} \quad \text{or} \quad \vec{F} = m\vec{a}$$

The acceleration $\vec{a}$ has the same direction as the resultant force $\vec{F}$.

The vector equation $\vec{F} = m\vec{a}$ can be written in terms of components as

$$\Sigma F_x = ma_x \qquad \Sigma F_y = ma_y \qquad \Sigma F_z = ma_z$$

where the forces are the components of the external forces acting on the object.

Newton's Third Law: Matter *interacts* with matter—forces come in pairs. *For each force exerted on one body, there is an equal, but oppositely directed, force on some other body interacting with it.* This is often called the *Law of Action and Reaction*.

The Law of Universal Gravitation

When two masses m and m´ gravitationally interact, they attract each other with forces of equal magnitude. For point masses (or spherically symmetric bodies), the attractive force F_G is given by

$$F_G = G\frac{mm´}{r^2}$$

where r is the distance between mass centers, and where $G = 6.67 \times 10^{-11}$ N m²/kg² when F_G is in newtons, m and m´ are in kilograms, and r is in meters.

Weight

The weight of an object (F_W) is the gravitational force acting downward on the object. On the Earth, it is the gravitational force exerted on the object by the planet. Its units are newtons (in the SI) and pounds (in the British system). An object of mass m falling freely toward the Earth is subject to only one force—the pull of gravity, which we call the weight F_W of the object. The object's acceleration due to F_W is the free-fall acceleration g.

Therefore, $F = ma$ provides us with the relation between $F = F_W$, $a = g$, and m; it is $F_W = mg$. Because, on average, $g = 9.8$ m/s² on Earth, a 1.0-kg object weighs 9.8 N at the Earth's surface.

Specific Types of Forces

The **tensile force** ($\vec{F}_T$) acting on a string, chain, or tendon is the applied force tending to stretch it. The magnitude of the tensile force is the **tension** (F_T).

The **normal force** ($\vec{F}_N$) on an object that is being supported by a surface is the component of the supporting force that is perpendicular to the surface.

The **friction force** ($\vec{F}_f$) is a tangential force acting on an object that opposes the sliding of that object on an adjacent surface with which it is in contact. The friction force is parallel to the surface and opposite to the direction of motion or of impending motion. Only when the applied force exceeds the maximum static friction force will an object begin to slide.

The **coefficient of kinetic friction** (μ_k), defined for the case in which one surface is sliding across another at constant speed, is

$$\mu_k = \frac{\text{friction force}}{\text{normal force}} = \frac{F_f}{F_N}$$

The **coefficient of static friction** (μ_s), defined for the case in which one surface is just on the verge of sliding across another surface, is

$$\mu_s = \frac{\text{maximum friction force}}{\text{normal force}} = \frac{F_f(\text{max})}{F_N}$$

where the maximum friction force occurs when the object is just on the verge of slipping but is nonetheless at rest.

Dimensional Analysis

All mechanical quantities, such as acceleration and force, can be expressed in terms of three fundamental dimensions: length L, mass M, and time T. For example, acceleration is a length (a distance) divided by (time)^2; we say it has the dimensions L/T^2, which we write as [LT^{-2}].

The dimensions of volume are [L^3], and those of velocity are [LT^{-1}]. Because force is mass multiplied by acceleration, its dimensions are [MLT^{-2}]. Dimensions are helpful in checking equations, since each term of an equation must have the same dimensions. For example,

$$s = v_1 t + \frac{1}{2} at^2$$

$$[L] \rightarrow [LT^{-1}][T] + [LT^{-2}][T^2]$$

so each term has the dimensions of length. As examples, an equation cannot have a volume [L^3] added to an area [L^2], or a force [MLT^{-2}] subtracted from a velocity [LT^{-1}]; these terms do not have the same dimensions.

Remember, all terms in an equation must have the same dimensions.

Mathematical Operations with Units

In every mathematical operation, the units terms (for example, lb, cm, ft^3, mi/h, m/s^2) must be carried along with the numbers and must undergo the same mathematical operations as the numbers.

Quantities cannot be added or subtracted directly unless they have the same units (as well as the same dimensions). For example, if we are to add algebraically 5 m (length) and 8 cm (length), we must first convert m to cm or cm to m. However, quantities of any sort can be combined in multiplication or division, in which the units as well as the numbers obey the algebraic laws of squaring, cancellation, etc.

Equilibrium under the Action of Concurrent Forces

Concurrent Forces

Concurrent forces are forces whose lines of action all pass through a common point. The forces acting on a point object are concurrent because they all pass through the same point, the point object.

Equilibrium

An object is in **equilibrium** under the action of concurrent forces provided it is not accelerating. A condition for equilibrium under concurrent forces is the requirement that $\Sigma \vec{F} = 0$ or, in component form,

$$\Sigma F_x = \Sigma F_y = \Sigma F_z = 0$$

That is, the resultant of all external forces acting on the object must be zero.

Problem Solution Method (Concurrent Forces)

(1) Isolate the object for discussion.
(2) Show the forces acting on the isolated object in a diagram (the *free-body* diagram).
(3) Find the rectangular components of each force.
(4) Write the condition for equilibrium in equation form.
(5) Solve for the required quantities.

Equilibrium of a Rigid Body Under Coplanar Forces

The **torque (or moment)** about an axis, due to a force, is a measure of the effectiveness of the force in producing rotation about that axis. It is defined in the following way:

Torque $= \tau = rF \sin \theta$

where r is the radial distance from the axis to the point of application of the force, and θ is the acute angle between the lines-of-action of $\vec{r}$ and $\vec{F}$, as shown in Figure 1-5.

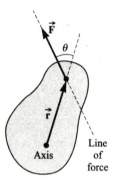

Figure 1-5

Often this definition is written in terms of the lever arm of the force, which is the perpendicular distance from the axis to the line of the force, as shown in Figure 1-6.

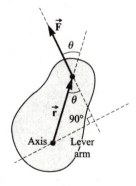

Figure 1-6

Because the lever arm is simply r sin θ, the torque becomes

$$\tau = (F)(\text{lever arm})$$

The units of torque are newton-meters (N • m). Plus and minus signs can be assigned to torques; for example, a torque that tends to cause counterclockwise rotation about the axis is positive, whereas one causing clockwise rotation is negative.

Conditions for Equilibrium

The two conditions for equilibrium of a rigid object under the action of *coplanar forces* are:

(1) As listed above, the first condition for equilibrium is the *force condition.*

The vector sum of all forces acting on the body must be zero:

$$\Sigma F_x = 0 \quad \text{and} \quad \Sigma F_y = 0$$

where the plane of the coplanar forces is taken to be the xy-plane.

(2) The second condition for equilibrium is the **torque condition.**

Take an axis perpendicular to the plane of the coplanar forces. Call the torques that tend to cause clockwise rotation about the axis negative, and counterclockwise torques positive; then the sum of all the torques acting on the object must be zero:

$$\Sigma \tau = 0$$

If the sum of the torques is zero about one axis for a body that obeys the force condition, it is zero about all other axes parallel to the first. We can choose the axis in such a way that the line of an unknown force passes through the intersection of the axis and the plane of the forces. The angle θ between $\vec{r}$ and $\vec{F}$ is then zero; hence, that particular unknown force exerts zero torque and therefore does not appear in the torque equation.

Essential Point

Center of Gravity

The **center of gravity** of an object is the point at which the entire weight of the object may be concentrated; i.e., the line-of-action of the weight passes through the center of gravity. A single vertically upward directed force, equal in magnitude to the weight of the object and applied through its center of gravity, will keep the object in equilibrium.

Work, Energy, and Power

Work

The work done by a force is defined as the product of that force times the parallel distance over which it acts. Consider the simple case of straight-line motion shown in Figure 1-7, where a force $\vec{F}$ acts on a body that simultaneously undergoes a vector displacement $\vec{s}$. The component of $\vec{F}$ in the direction of $\vec{s}$ is $F \cos \theta$. The work W done by the force $\vec{F}$ is defined to be the component of $\vec{F}$ in the direction of the displacement, multiplied by the displacement:

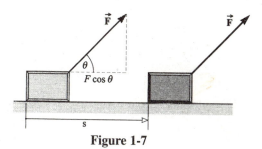

Figure 1-7

$W = (F \cos \theta)(s) = Fs \cos \theta$

Notice that θ is the angle between the force and displacement vectors. Work is a scalar quantity. The SI unit of work is the newton-meter, called the joule (J). One joule is the work done by a force of 1 N when it displaces an object 1 m in the direction of the force. Other units sometimes used for work are the erg, where 1 erg $= 10^{-7}$ J, and the foot-pound (ft-lb), where 1 ft-lb = 1.355 J.

If $\vec{F}$ and $\vec{s}$ are in the same direction, $\cos \theta = \cos 0° = 1$ and $W = Fs$. But, if $\vec{F}$ and $\vec{s}$ are in opposite directions, then $\cos \theta = \cos 180° = -1$ and $W = -Fs$; the work is negative. Forces such as friction often slow the motion of an object and are then opposite in direction to the displacement. Such forces usually do negative work.

Work is the transfer of energy from one entity to another by way of the action of a force applied over a distance. The point of application of the force must move if work is to be done.

Energy

Energy is a measure of the change imparted to a system. It is given to an object when a force does work on the object. The amount of energy transferred to the object equals the work done. Further, when an object does work, it loses an amount of energy equal to the work it does. Energy and work have the same units, joules. Energy, like work, is a scalar quantity. An object that is capable of doing work possesses energy.

Kinetic energy (KE) is the energy possessed by an object because it is in motion. If an object of mass m is moving with a speed v, it has translational KE given by

$$KE = \frac{1}{2}mv^2$$

When m is in kg and v is in m/s, the units of KE are joules.

Gravitational potential energy (GPE) is the energy possessed by an object because of the gravitational interaction. As mass falls through a vertical distance h, a gravitational force can do work in the amount mgh. We define the

GPE of an object relative to an arbitrary zero level, often the Earth's surface. If the object is at a height h above the zero (or reference) level, its GPE is

GPE = mgh

where g is the acceleration due to gravity. Notice that mg is the weight of the object. The units of GPE are joules when m is in kg, g is in m/s^2, and h is in m.

Work-Energy Theorem

When work is done on a point mass or a rigid body, and there is no change in PE, the energy imparted can only appear as KE. Insofar as a body is not totally rigid, however, energy can be transferred to its parts and the work done on it will not precisely equal its change in KE.

Conservation of Energy

Energy can be neither created nor destroyed, but only transformed from one kind to another.

Power

Power is the time rate of doing work:

$$\text{Average power} = \frac{\text{work done by a force}}{\text{time taken to do this work}} = \text{force} \times \text{speed}$$

where the speed is measured in the direction of the force applied to the object. More generally, power is the rate of transfer of energy. In the SI, the unit of power is the watt (W), and 1 W = 1 J/s. Another unit of power often used is the horsepower: 1 hp = 746 W.

Impulse and Momentum

Linear Momentum

The **linear momentum** ($\vec{P}$) of a body is the product of its mass (m) and velocity ($\vec{v}$):

Linear momentum = (mass of body)(velocity of body)

$$\vec{p} = m\vec{v}$$

Momentum is a vector quantity whose direction is that of the velocity. The SI units of momentum are kg • m/s.

Impulse

An **impulse** is the product of a force ($\vec{F}$) and the time interval (Δt) over which the force acts:

Impulse = (force)(length of time the force acts)

Impulse is a vector quantity whose direction is that of the force. Its SI units are N • s.

An impulse causes a change in momentum. The change of momentum produced by an impulse is equal to the impulse in both magnitude and direction. Thus, if a constant force $\vec{F}$ acting for a time Δt on a body of mass m changes its velocity from an initial value $\vec{v}_i$ to a final value $\vec{v}_f$, then

Impulse = change in momentum

$$\vec{F}\,\Delta t = m\left(\vec{v}_f - \vec{v}_i\right)$$

> # Remember!
>
> ## Conservation of Linear Momentum
>
> If the net external force acting on a system of objects is zero, the vector sum of the momenta of the objects will remain constant.

Newton's Second Law was actually given as $\vec{F} = \dfrac{\Delta \vec{p}}{\Delta t}$ from which it follows that $\vec{F}\Delta t = \Delta \vec{p}$. Moreover, $\vec{F}\Delta t = \Delta(m\vec{v})$, and if m is constant $\vec{F}\Delta t = m(\vec{v}_f - \vec{v}_i)$.

Collisions and Explosions

In **collisions and explosions**, the vector sum of the momenta just before the event equals the vector sum of the momenta just after the event. The vector sum of the momenta of the objects involved does not change during the collision or explosion. Thus, when two bodies of masses m_1 and m_2 collide,

Total momentum before impact = total momentum after impact

$$m_1\vec{u}_1 + m_2\vec{u}_2 = m_1\vec{v}_1 + m_2\vec{v}_2$$

where $\vec{u}_1$ and $\vec{u}_2$ are the velocities before impact, and $\vec{v}_1$ and $\vec{v}_2$ are the velocities after impact. In one dimension, in component form,

$$m_1 u_{1x} + m_2 u_{2x} = m_1 v_{1x} + m_2 v_{2x}$$

and similarly for the y- and z-components. Remember that vector quantities are always boldfaced and velocity is a vector. On the other hand, u_{1x}, u_{2x}, v_{1x}, and v_{2x} are the scalar values of the velocities (they can be positive or negative). A positive direction is initially selected and vectors pointing opposite to this have negative numerical scalar values.

A **perfectly elastic collision** is one in which the sum of the translational KEs of the objects is not changed during the collision. In the case of two bodies,

$$\frac{1}{2}m_1u_1^2 + \frac{1}{2}m_2u_2^2 = \frac{1}{2}m_1v_1^2 + \frac{1}{2}m_2v_2^2$$

Coefficient of Restitution

For any collision between two bodies in which the bodies move only along a single straight line (e.g., the x-axis), a **coefficient of restitution**, **e**, is defined. It is a pure number given by

$$e = \frac{v_{2x} - v_{1x}}{u_{1x} - u_{2x}}$$

where u_{1x} and u_{2x} are values before impact, and v_{1x} and v_{2x} are values after impact. Notice that $|u_{1x} - u_{2x}|$ is the relative speed of approach and $|v_{2x} - v_{1x}|$ is the relative speed of recession.

For a perfectly elastic collision, $e = 1$. For inelastic collisions, $e < 1$. If the bodies stick together after collision, $e = 0$.

Center of Mass

The **center of mass** of an object (of mass m) is the single point that moves in the same way as a point mass (of mass m) would move when subjected to the same external forces that act on the object. That is, if the resultant force acting on an object (or system of objects) of mass m is $\vec{F}$, the acceleration of the center of mass of the object (or system) is given by

$$\vec{a}_{cm} = \frac{\vec{F}}{m}$$

If the object is considered to be composed of tiny masses m_1, m_2, m_3, and so on, at coordinates (x_1, y_1, z_1), (x_2, y_2, z_2), and so on, then the coordinates of the center of mass are given by

$$x_{cm} = \frac{\Sigma x_i m_i}{\Sigma m_i}, \quad y_{cm} = \frac{\Sigma y_i m_i}{\Sigma m_i}, \quad z_{cm} = \frac{\Sigma z_i m_i}{\Sigma m_i}$$

where the sums extend over all masses composing the object. In a uniform gravitational field, the center of mass and the center of gravity coincide.

Angular Motion in a Plane

Angular Displacement

Angular displacement (θ) is usually expressed in radians, in degrees, or in revolutions:

$$1 \text{ rev} = 360^o = 2\pi \text{ rad} \qquad \text{or} \qquad 1 \text{ rad} = 57.3^o$$

One radian is the angle subtended at the center of a circle by an arc equal in length to the radius of the circle. Thus an angle θ in radians is given in terms of the arc length l it subtends on a circle of radius r by:

$$\theta = \frac{l}{r}$$

The radian measure of an angle is a dimensionless number. Radians, like degrees, are not a physical unit—the radian is not expressible in meters, kilograms, or seconds. Nonetheless, we will use the abbreviation rad to remind us that we are working with radians.

Angular Speed

The angular speed (ω) of an object whose axis of rotation is fixed is the rate at which its angular coordinate, the angular displacement θ, changes with time. If θ changes from θ_i to θ_f in a time t, then the *average angular speed* is

$$\omega_{av} = \frac{\theta_f - \theta_i}{t}$$

The units of ω_{av} are exclusively rad/s. Since each complete turn or cycle of a revolving system carries it through 2π rad,

$$\omega = 2\pi f$$

where f is the **frequency** in revolutions per second, rotations per second, or cycles per second. Accordingly, ω is also called the **angular frequency**. We can associate a direction with ω and thereby create a vector quantity $\vec{\omega}$. Thus, if the fingers of the right hand curve around in the direction of rotation, the thumb points along the axis of rotation in the direction of $\vec{\omega}$, the **angular velocity** vector.

Angular Acceleration

The angular acceleration (α) of an object whose axis of rotation is fixed is the rate at which its angular speed changes with time. If ω changes uniformly from ω_i to ω_f in a time t, then the *angular acceleration* is constant and

$$\alpha = \frac{\omega_f - \omega_i}{t}$$

The units of α are typically rad/s^2, rev/min^2, and such.

Equations for Uniformly Accelerated Angular Motion

The equations for uniformly accelerated angular motion are exactly analogous to those for uniformly accelerated linear motion. In the usual notation, we have:

Linear	Angular
$v_{av} = \dfrac{1}{2}\left(v_i + v_f\right)$	$\omega_{av} = \dfrac{1}{2}\left(\omega_i + \omega_f\right)$
$s = v_{av}t$	$\theta = \omega_{av}t$
$v_f = v_i + at$	$\omega_f = \omega_i + \alpha t$
$v_f^2 = v_i^2 + 2as$	$\omega_f^2 = \omega_i^2 + 2\alpha\theta$
$s = v_i t + \dfrac{1}{2}at^2$	$\theta = \omega_i t + \dfrac{1}{2}\alpha t^2$

Taken alone, the second of these equations is just the definition of average speed, so it is valid whether the acceleration is constant or not.

Relation Between Angular and Tangential Quantities

When a wheel of radius r rotates about an axis whose direction is fixed, a point on the rim of the wheel is described in terms of the circumferential distance l it has moved, its tangential speed v, and its tangential acceleration, a_T. These quantities are related to the angular quantities θ, ω, and α, which describe the rotation of the wheel, through the relations

$$l = r\theta \qquad\qquad v = r\omega \qquad\qquad a_T = r\alpha$$

provided radian measure is used for θ, ω, and α. By simple reasoning, l can be shown to be the length of belt wound on the wheel or the distance the wheel would roll (without slipping) if free to do so. In such cases, v and a_T refer to the tangential speed and acceleration of a point on the belt or of the center of the wheel.

Centripetal Acceleration

A point mass m moving with constant speed v around a circle of radius r is undergoing acceleration. Although the magnitude of its linear velocity is not changing, the direction of the velocity is continually changing. This change in velocity gives rise to an acceleration a_C of the mass, directed toward the center of the circle. We call this acceleration the **centripetal acceleration**; its magnitude is given by

$$a_c = \frac{(\text{tangential speed})^2}{\text{radius of circular path}} = \frac{v^2}{r}$$

where v is the speed of the mass around the perimeter of the circle.

Because $v = r\omega$, we also have $a_c = r\omega^2$, where ω must be in rad/s. Notice that the word "acceleration" is commonly used in physics as either a scalar or a vector quantity. Fortunately, there is usually no ambiguity.

Centripetal Force

The **centripetal force** ($\vec{F}_c$) is the force that must act on a mass m moving in a circular path of radius r to give it the centripetal acceleration v^2/r. From F = ma, we have

$$F_c = \frac{mv^2}{r} = mr\omega^2$$

where $\vec{F}_c$ is directed toward the center of the circular path.

Rigid-Body Rotation

Moment of Inertia

The **moment of inertia** (I) of a body is a measure of the rotational inertia of the body. If an object that is free to rotate about an axis is difficult to set into rotation, its moment of inertia about that axis is large. An object with small I has little rotational inertia.

If a body is considered to be made up of tiny masses m_1, m_2, m_3, . . . , at respective distances r_1, r_2, r_3, . . . , from an axis, its moment of inertia about the axis is

$$I = m_1 r_1^2 + m_2 r_2^2 + m_3 r_3^2 + \cdots = \sum m_i r_i^2$$

The units of I are kg • m².

It is convenient to define a **radius of gyration** (**k**) for an object about an axis by the relation

$$I = Mk^2$$

where M is the total mass of the object. Hence k is the distance a point mass M must be from the axis if the point mass is to have the same I as the object.

Torque and Angular Acceleration

A torque τ acting on a body of moment of inertia I produces in it an angular acceleration α given by

$$\tau = I\alpha$$

Here, τ is in N • m, I is in kg • m², and α must be in rad/s².

Kinetic Energy of Rotation

The **kinetic energy of rotation** (**KE$_r$**) of a mass whose moment of inertia about an axis is I, and which is rotating about the axis with angular velocity ω, is

$$KE_r = \frac{1}{2} I\omega^2$$

where the energy is in joules and ω must be in rad/s.

Combined Rotation and Translation

The KE of a rolling ball or other rolling object of mass M is the sum of (1) its rotational KE *about an axis through its center of mass* and (2) the translational KE of an equivalent point mass moving with the center of mass. In symbols,

$$KE_{total} = \frac{1}{2}I\omega^2 + \frac{1}{2}Mv^2$$

Note that I is the moment of inertia of the object about an axis through its mass center.

Rotational Work

The work (W) done on a rotating body during an angular displacement θ by a constant torque τ is given by

$$W = \tau\theta$$

where W is in joules and θ must be in radians.

Rotational Power

The power (P) transmitted to a body by a torque is given by

$$P = \tau\omega$$

where τ is the applied torque about the axis of rotation, and ω is the angular speed about that same axis. Radian measure must be used for ω.

Angular Impulse

Angular impulse has magnitude τt, where t is the time during which the constant torque τ acts on the object. In analogy to the linear case, an angular impulse τt on a body causes a change in angular momentum of the body given by

Important Point!

Angular Momentum

Angular momentum is a vector quantity that has magnitude I ω and is directed along the axis of rotation. If the net torque on a body is zero, its angular momentum will remain unchanged in both magnitude and direction. This is the *Law of Conservation of Angular Momentum.*

$$\tau t = I\omega_f - I\omega_i$$

Parallel-Axis Theorem

The moment of inertia I of a body about an axis parallel to an axis through the center of mass is

$$I = I_{cm} + Mh^2$$

where I_{cm} = moment of inertia about an axis through the center of mass

   M = total mass of the body

   h = perpendicular distance between the two parallel axes

The moments of inertia (about an axis through the center of mass) of several uniform objects, each of mass M, are shown in Figure 1-8.

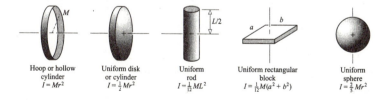

Hoop or hollow cylinder
$I = Mr^2$

Uniform disk or cylinder
$I = \frac{1}{2}Mr^2$

Uniform rod
$I = \frac{1}{12}ML^2$

Uniform rectangular block
$I = \frac{1}{12}M(a^2 + b^2)$

Uniform sphere
$I = \frac{2}{5}Mr^2$

Figure 1-8

Analogous Linear and Angular Quantities

Linear displacement, s	↔	Angular displacement, θ
Linear speed, v	↔	Angular speed, ω
Linear acceleration, a_T	↔	Angular acceleration, α
Mass (inertia), m	↔	Moment of inertia, I
Force, F	↔	Torque, τ
Linear momentum, mv	↔	Angular momentum, Iω
Linear impulse, Ft	↔	Angular impulse, τt

If, in the equations for linear motion, we replace linear quantities by the corresponding angular quantities, we get the corresponding equations for angular motion. Thus, we have

Linear. $F=ma;$ $KE=\dfrac{1}{2}mv^2;$ $W=Fs;$ $P=Fv$

Angular. $\tau=I\alpha;$ $KE_r=\dfrac{1}{2}I\omega^2;$ $W=\tau\theta;$ $P=\tau\omega$

In these equations, θ, ω, and α must be expressed in radian measure.

Solved Problems

Solved Problem 1.1 The five coplanar forces shown in Figure SP1-1 act on an object. Find their resultant.

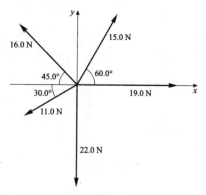

Figure SP1-1

Solution. (1) First we find the x- and y-components of each force. These components are as follows:

Force	x-Component	y-Component
19.0 N	19.0 N	0 N
15.0 N	(15.0 N) cos 60.0° = 7.50 N	(15.0 N) sin 60.0° = 13.0 N
16.0 N	-(16.0 N) cos 45.0° = -11.3 N	(16.0 N) sin 45.0° = 11.3 N
11.0 N	-(11.0 N) cos 30.0° = -9.53 N	-(11.0 N) sin 30.0° = -5.50
22.0 N	0 N	N

Note the + and - signs to indicate direction.

(2) The resultant **R** has components $R_x = \Sigma F_x$ and $R_y = \Sigma F_y$, where we read ΣF_x as "the sum of all the x-force components." We then have

$R_x = 19.0 + 7.5 - 11.3 - 9.5 + 0 = +5.7$ N
$R_y = 0 + 13.0 + 11.3 - 5.5 - 22.0 = -3.2$ N

(3) The magnitude of the resultant is

$$R = \sqrt{R_x^2 + R_y^2} = 6.5 \text{ N}$$

(4) Finally, we sketch the resultant as shown in Figure SP1-2. And find its angle. We see that

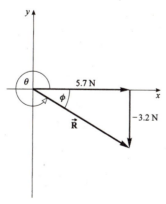

Figure SP1-2

$$\tan \phi = \frac{3.2}{5.7} = 0.56$$

from which $\phi = 29^0$. Then, $\theta = 360^0 - 29^0 = 331^0$. The resultant is 6.5 N at 331° (or - 29°).

Solved Problem 1.2   A rope extends between two poles. A 90 N boy hangs from it as shown in Figure SP1-3. Find the tensions in the two parts of the rope.

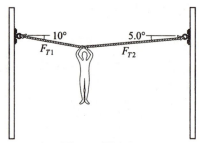

Figure SP1-3

Solution. We label the two tensions T_1 and T_2, and isolate the rope at the boy's hands as the object. The free-body diagram for the object is shown in Figure SP1-4.

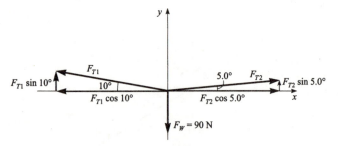

Figure SP1-4

After resolving the forces into their components as shown, we can write the first condition for equilibrium:

$\Sigma F_x = 0$ becomes $T_2 \cos 5^0 - T_1 \cos 10^0 = 0$

$\Sigma F_y = 0$ becomes $T_2 \sin 5^0 + T_1 \sin 10^\circ - 90\ N = 0$

When we evaluate the sines and cosines, these equations become

$0.996\ T_2 - 0.985\ T_1 = 0$ and $0.087\ T_2 + 0.174\ T_1 - 90 = 0$

Solving the first for T_2 gives $T_2 = 0.990\ T_1$. Substituting this in the second equation gives

$0.086\ T_1 + 0.174\ T_1 - 90 = 0$

from which $T_1 = 346\ N$. Then, because $T_2 = 0.990\ T_1$, we have $T_2 = 343\ N$.

Solved Problem 1.3 A baseball is thrown with an initial velocity of 100 m/s at an angle of 30^0 above the horizontal, as shown in Figure SP1-5. How far from the throwing point will the baseball attain its original level?

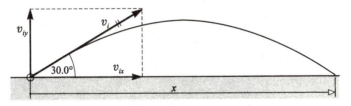

Figure SP1-5

Solution. We divide the problem into horizontal and vertical parts, for which

$v_{ox} = v_o \cos 30^\circ = 86.6\ m/s$ and $v_{ox} = v_o \sin 30^\circ = 50\ m/s$

where *up* is taken as positive.

In the vertical problem, y = 0 since the ball returns to its original height. Then

$$y=v_{oy}t+\frac{1}{2}a_yt^2 \text{ or } 0=(50 \text{ m/s})+\frac{1}{2}(-9.8 \text{ m/s}^2)t$$

and t = 10.2 s.

In the horizontal problem, $v_{ox} = v_{fx} = \bar{v}_x = 86.6$ m/s. Therefore,

$$x=\bar{v}_xt=(86.6 \text{ m/s})(10.2 \text{ s})=884 \text{ m}$$

Solved Problem 1.4 A 600 N object is to be given an acceleration of 0.70 m/s². How large an unbalanced force must act upon it?

Solution. Notice that the weight, not the mass, of the object is given. Assuming the weight was measured on the earth, we use W = mg to find

$$m=\frac{W}{g}=\frac{600 \text{ N}}{9.8 \text{ m/s}^2}=61 \text{ kg}$$

Now that we know the mass of the object (61 kg) and the desired acceleration (0.70 m/s²), we have

F = ma = (61 kg)(0.70 m/s²) = 43 N.

Solved Problem 1.5 A ladder leans against a smooth wall, as shown in Figure SP1-6. (By a "smooth" wall, we mean that the wall exerts on the ladder only a force that is perpendicular to the wall. There is no friction force.) The ladder weighs 200 N and its center of gravity is 0.4L from the base, where L is the ladder's length. (a) How large a friction force must exist at the base of the ladder if it is not to slip? (b) What is the necessary coefficient of static friction?

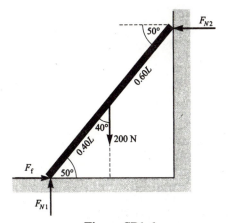

Figure SP1-6

Solution. (a) We wish to find the friction force H. Notice that no friction force exists at the top of the ladder. Taking torques about point A gives the torque equation

$$- (0.4L)(200\ N)(\sin 40°) + (L)(P)(\sin 50°) = 0$$

Solving gives P = 67.1 N. We can also write

$$\sum F_x = 0 \quad \text{or} \quad H - P = 0$$

$$\sum F_y = 0 \quad \text{or} \quad V - 200 = 0$$

and so H = 67.1 N and V = 200 N.

(b)

$$\mu_s = \frac{f}{F_N} = \frac{H}{V} = \frac{67.1}{200} = 0.34$$

Solved Problem 1.6 The graph of an object's motion along a line is shown in Figure SP1-7. Find the instantaneous velocity of the object at points A and B. What is the object's average velocity? Its acceleration?

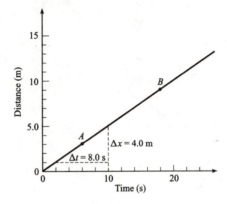

Figure SP1-7

Solution. Because the velocity is given by the slope $\Delta x/\Delta t$ of the tangent line, we take a tangent to the curve at point A. The tangent line is the curve itself in this case. For the triangle shown at A, we have

$$\frac{\Delta x}{\Delta t} = \frac{4 \text{ m}}{8 \text{ s}} = 0.50 \text{ m/s}$$

This is also the velocity at point B and at every other point on the straight-line graph. It follows that $a = 0$ and $\bar{v}_x = v_x = 0.50$ m/s.

Chapter 2
DENSITY, ELASTICITY, AND FLUIDS

IN THIS CHAPTER:

✔ *Simple Harmonic Motion and Springs*
✔ *Density and Elasticity*
✔ *Fluids at Rest*
✔ *Fluids in Motion*
✔ *Solved Problems*

Simple Harmonic Motion and Springs

Period

The **period** (**T**) of a cyclic system, one that is vibrating or rotating in a repetitive fashion, is the time required for the system to complete one full cycle. In the case of vibration, it is the total time for the combined back and forth motion of the system. The period is the *number of seconds per cycle.*

Frequency

The **frequency (f)** is the number of vibrations made per unit time or *the number of cycles per second*. Because T is the time for one cycle, f = 1/T. The unit of frequency is the *hertz,* where one cycle/s is one hertz (Hz).

The graph of a vibratory motion, shown in Figure 2-1, depicts up-and-down oscillation of a mass at the end of a spring. One complete cycle is from a to b, or from c to d, or from e to f. The time taken for one cycle is T, the period.

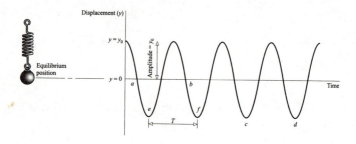

Figure 2-1

Displacement

The **displacement** (x or y) is the distance of the vibrating object from its equilibrium position (normal rest position), i.e., from the center of its vibration path. The maximum displacement is called the amplitude (see Figure 2-1).

Restoring Force

A **restoring force** is one that opposes the displacement of the system; it is necessary if vibration is to occur. In other words, a restoring force is always directed so as to push or pull the system back to its equilibrium (normal rest) position. For a mass at the end of a spring, the stretched spring pulls the mass back toward the equilibrium position, while the compressed spring pushes the mass back toward the equilibrium position.

Simple Harmonic Motion

Simple harmonic motion (**SHM**) is the vibratory motion which a system that obeys Hooke's Law undergoes. The motion illustrated in Figure 2-1 is SHM. Because of the resemblance of its graph to a sine or cosine curve, SHM is frequently called *sinusoidal motion*. A central feature of SHM is that the system oscillates at a single constant frequency. That's what makes it "simple" harmonic.

Hooke's Law

A Hookean system (a spring, wire, rod, etc.) is one that returns to its original configuration after being distorted and then released. Moreover, when such a system is stretched a distance x (for compression, x is negative), the restoring force exerted by the spring is given by **Hooke's Law**:

$$F = -kx$$

The minus sign indicates that the restoring force is always opposite in direction to the displacement. The **spring constant k** has units of N/m and is a measure of the stiffness of the spring. Most springs obey Hooke's Law for small distortions.

It is sometimes useful to express Hooke's Law in terms of F_{ext}, the external force needed to stretch the spring a given amount x. This force is the negative of the restoring force, and so

$$F_{ext} = kx$$

Elastic Potential Energy

The **elastic potential energy** stored in a Hookean spring (EPE) that is distorted a distance x is $\frac{1}{2}kx^2$. If the amplitude of motion is x_0 for a mass at the end of a spring, then the energy of the vibrating system is $\frac{1}{2}kx_0^2$ at all times. However, this energy is completely stored in the spring only when $x = \pm x_0$, that is, when the mass has its maximum displacement.

Conservation of Energy

Energy interchange between kinetic and potential energy occurs constantly in a vibrating system. When the system passes through its equilibrium position, KE = maximum and EPE = 0. When the system has its maximum displacement, then KE = 0 and EPE = maximum. From the law of conservation of energy, in the absence of friction-type losses,

KE + EPE = constant

For a mass m at the end of a spring (whose own mass is negligible), this becomes

$$\frac{1}{2}mv^2 + \frac{1}{2}kx^2 = \frac{1}{2}kx_0^2$$

where x_0 is the amplitude of the motion.

Motion in SHM

The speed in SHM is determined via the above energy equation as

$$|v| = \sqrt{(x_0^2 - x^2)\frac{k}{m}}$$

Acceleration in SHM is determined via Hooke's Law, $F = -kx$, and $F = ma$; once displaced and released, the restoring force drives the system. Equating these two expressions for F gives

$$a = -\frac{k}{m}x$$

The minus sign indicates that the direction of $\vec{a}$ (and $\vec{F}$) is always opposite to the direction of the displacement $\vec{x}$. Keep in mind that neither $\vec{F}$ nor $\vec{a}$ is constant.

Reference Circle

Suppose that a point P moves with constant speed v_0 around a circle, as shown in Figure 2-2.

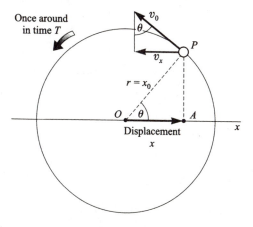

Figure 2-2

This circle is called the **reference circle** for SHM. Point A is the projection of point P on the x-axis, which coincides with the horizontal diameter of the circle. The motion of point A back and forth about point O as center is SHM. The amplitude of the motion is x_0, the radius of the circle. The time taken for P to go around the circle once is the period T of the motion. The velocity, $\vec{v}_0$, of point A has a scalar component of

$$v_x = - v_0 \sin \theta$$

When this quantity is positive, $\vec{v}_x$, points in the positive x-direction; when it's negative, $\vec{v}_x$ points in the negative x-direction.

Period in SHM

The **period T** of a SHM is the time taken for point P to go once around the reference circle in Figure 2-2. Therefore,

$$T=\frac{2\pi r}{v_0}=\frac{2\pi x_0}{v_0}$$

But v_0 is the maximum speed of point A in Figure 2-2, that is, v_0 is the value of $|v_x|$ in SHM when $x = 0$:

$$|v_x|=\sqrt{(x_0^2-x^2)\frac{k}{m}}\quad\text{gives}\quad v_0=x_0\sqrt{\frac{k}{m}}$$

This then gives the period of SHM to be

$$T=2\pi\sqrt{\frac{m}{k}}$$

for a Hookean spring system. Eliminating the quantity k/m between the two equations $a = -(k/m)x$ and $T=2\pi\sqrt{m/k}$, we find

$$a=-\frac{4\pi^2}{T^2}x$$

Simple Pendulum

The simple pendulum very nearly undergoes SHM if its angle of swing is not too large. The period of vibration for a pendulum of length L at a location where the gravitational acceleration is g is given by

$$T=2\pi\sqrt{\frac{L}{g}}$$

SHM can be expressed in analytic form by reference to Figure 2-2, where we see that the horizontal displacement of point P is given by $x = x_0 \cos \theta$. Since $\theta = \omega t = 2\pi ft$, where the **angular frequency** $\omega = 2\pi f$ is the angular velocity of the reference point on the circle, we have

$$x = x_0 \cos 2\pi ft = x_0 \cos \omega t$$

Similarly, the vertical component of the motion of point P is given by

$$y = x_0 \sin 2\pi ft = x_0 \sin \omega t$$

Also, from the figure, $v_x = v_0 \sin 2\pi ft$.

Density and Elasticity

Mass Density

The **mass density** (ρ) of a material is its mass per unit volume:

$$\rho = \frac{\text{mass of body}}{\text{volume of body}} = \frac{m}{V}$$

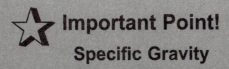

⭐ Important Point!
Specific Gravity

The **specific gravity** (sp gr) of a substance is the ratio of the density of the substance to the density of some standard substance. The standard is usually water (at 4°C) for liquids and solids, while for gases, it is usually air.

$$sp\ gr = \frac{\rho}{\rho_{standard}}$$

Since sp gr is a dimensionless ratio, it has the same value for all systems of units.

The SI unit for mass density is kg/m^3, although g/cm^3 is also used: 1000 $kg/m^3 = 1$ g/cm^3. The density of water is approximately 1000 kg/m^3.

Elasticity

Elasticity is the property by which a body returns to its original size and shape when the forces that deformed it are removed.

The **stress** (σ) experienced within a solid is the magnitude of the force acting (F), divided by the area (A) over which it acts:

$$\text{Stress} = \frac{\text{force}}{\text{area of surface on which force acts}}$$

$$\sigma = \frac{F}{A}$$

Its SI unit is the pascal (Pa), where 1 $Pa = 1$ N/m^2. Thus, if a cane supports a load, the stress at any point within the cane is the load divided by the cross-sectional area at that point; the narrowest regions experience the greatest stress.

Strain (ε) is the fractional deformation resulting from a stress. It is measured as the ratio of the change in some dimension of a body to the original dimension in which the change occurred.

$$\text{Strain} = \frac{\text{change in dimension}}{\text{original dimension}}$$

Thus, the normal strain under an axial load is the change in length (ΔL) over the original length L_0:

$$\varepsilon = \frac{\Delta L}{L_o}$$

Strain has no units because it is a ratio of like quantities. The exact definition of strain for various situations is given later.

> # Remember
>
> The **elastic limit** of a body is the smallest stress that will produce a permanent distortion in the body. When a stress in excess of this limit is applied, the body will not return exactly to its original state after the stress is removed.

Young's Modulus

Young's modulus (Y), or the modulus of elasticity, is defined as

$$\text{Modulus of elasticity} = \frac{\text{stress}}{\text{strain}}$$

The modulus has the same units as stress. A large modulus means that a large stress is required to produce a given strain—the object is rigid. Accordingly,

$$Y = \frac{F/A}{\Delta L/L} = \frac{FL_o}{A\,\Delta L}$$

Its SI unit is Pa. Unlike the constant k in Hooke's Law, the value of Y depends only on the material of the wire or rod, and not on its dimensions or configuration. Consequently, Young's modulus is an important basic measure of the mechanical behavior of materials.

The **bulk modulus** (B) describes the volume elasticity of a material. Suppose that a uniformly distributed compressive force acts on the surface of an object and is directed perpendicular to the surface at all points. Then, if F is the force acting on and perpendicular to an area A, we define

$$\text{Pressure on A} = P = \frac{F}{A}$$

The SI unit for pressure is Pa.

Suppose that the pressure on an object of original volume V_0 is increased by an amount ΔP. The pressure increase causes a volume change ΔV, where ΔV will be negative. We then define

$$\text{Volume stress} = \Delta P \quad \text{Volume strain} = -\frac{\Delta V}{V_0}$$

$$\text{Bulk modulus} = \frac{\text{volume stress}}{\text{volume strain}}$$

$$B = -\frac{\Delta P}{\Delta V / V} = -\frac{V_0 \Delta P}{\Delta V}$$

The minus sign is used so as to cancel the negative numerical value of ΔV and thereby make B a positive number. The bulk modulus has the units of pressure. The reciprocal of the bulk modulus is called the **compressibility** K of the substance.

The **shear modulus** (S) describes the shape elasticity of a material. Suppose, as shown in Figure 2-3, that equal and opposite tangential forces F act on a rectangular block. These shearing forces distort the block as indicated, but its volume remains unchanged.

$$S = \frac{F}{A\gamma}$$

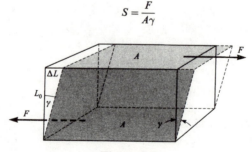

Figure 2-3

We define

Shearing stress = $\dfrac{\text{tangential force acting}}{\text{area of surface being sheared}}$

$$\sigma_s = \frac{F}{A}$$

Shearing strain = $\dfrac{\text{distance sheared}}{\text{distance between surfaces}}$

$$\varepsilon_s = \frac{\Delta L}{L_o}$$

Then

Shear modulus = $\dfrac{\text{shear stress}}{\text{shear strain}}$

$$S = \frac{F/A}{\Delta L/L_o} = \frac{FL_o}{A\,\Delta L}$$

Since ΔL is usually very small, the ratio $\Delta L/L_0$ is equal approximately to the shear angle γ in radians. In that case,

$$S = \frac{F}{A\gamma}$$

Fluids at Rest

The **average pressure** on a surface of area A is found as force divided by area, where it is stipulated that the force must be perpendicular (normal) to the area:

Average pressure = $\dfrac{\text{force acting normal to an area}}{\text{area over which the force is distributed}}$

$$P = \frac{F}{A}$$

Recall that the SI unit for pressure is the pascal (Pa), and 1 Pa = 1 N/m^2.

Standard atmospheric pressure is 1.01 x 10^5 Pa, and this is equivalent to 14.7 lb/in^2. Other units used for pressure are:

1 atmosphere (atm) = 1.013 × 10^5 Pa
1 torr = 1 mm of mercury (mmHg) = 133.32 Pa
1 lb/in^2 = 6.895 kPa

The **hydrostatic pressure** due to a column of fluid of height h and mass density ρ is

$$P = \rho g h$$

Pascal's Principle

When the pressure on any part of a confined fluid (liquid or gas) is changed, the pressure on every other part of the fluid is also changed by the same amount.

Archimedes' Principle

A body wholly or partly immersed in a fluid is buoyed up by a force equal to the weight of the fluid it displaces. The buoyant force can be considered to act vertically upward through the center of gravity of the displaced fluid.

F_B = buoyant force = weight of displaced fluid

The buoyant force on an object of volume V that is totally immersed in a fluid of density ρ_f is $\rho_f V g$, and the weight of the object is $\rho_0 V g$, where

ρ_0 is the density of the object. Therefore, the net upward force on the submerged object is

$$F_{net} \text{ (upward)} = Vg(\rho_f - \rho_0)$$

Fluids in Motion

Fluid flow

Fluid flow or discharge (J): When a fluid that fills a pipe flows through the pipe with an average speed v, the flow or discharge J is

$$J = Av$$

where A is the cross-sectional area of the pipe. The units of J are m³/s in the SI and ft³/s in U.S. customary units. Sometimes, J is called the **rate of flow** or the **discharge rate.**

Equation of Continuity

Suppose an **incompressible** (constant-density) fluid fills a pipe and flows through it. Suppose further that the cross-sectional area of the pipe is A_1 at one point and A_2 at another. Since the flow through A_1 must equal the flow through A_2, one has

$$J = A_1 v_1 = A_2 v_2 = \text{constant}$$

where v_1 and v_2 are the average fluid speeds over A_1 and A_2, respectively.

Shear Rate

The **shear rate** of a fluid is the rate at which the shear strain within the fluid is changing. Because strain has no units, the SI unit for shear rate is s^{-1}.

Viscosity

The **viscosity** (η) of a fluid is a measure of how large a shear stress is required to produce unit shear rate. Its unit is that of stress per unit shear rate, or Pa • s in the SI. Another SI unit is the N • s/m^2 (or kg/m • s), called the poiseuille (Pl): 1 Pl = 1 kg/m • s = 1 Pa • s. Other units used are the poise (P), where 1 P = 0.1 Pl, and the centipoise (cP), where 1 cP = 10^{-3} Pl. A viscous fluid, such as tar, has large η.

Poiseuille's Law

The fluid flow through a cylindrical pipe of length L and cross-sectional radius R is given by

$$J = \frac{\pi R^4 \left(P_i - P_o\right)}{8 \eta L}$$

where P_i - P_o is the pressure difference between the two ends of the pipe (input minus output).

Work Done by Pressure

The work done by a pressure P acting on a surface of area A as the surface moves through a distance Δx normal to the surface (thereby displacing a volume A Δx = ΔV) is

Work = PA Δx = P ΔV

Bernoulli's Equation

Bernoulli's equation for the steady flow of a continuous stream of fluid:

Consider two different points along the stream path. Let point 1 be at a height h_1 and let v_1, ρ_1, and P_1 be the fluid speed, density, and pressure at that point. Similarly define h_2, v_2, ρ_2, and P_2 for point 2. Then, provided the fluid is incompressible and has negligible viscosity,

$$P_1 + \frac{1}{2}\rho v_1^2 + h_1\rho g = P_2 + \frac{1}{2}\rho v_2^2 + h_2\rho g$$

where $\rho_1 = \rho_2 = \rho$ and g is the acceleration due to gravity.

Torricelli's Theorem

Suppose that a tank contains liquid and is open to the atmosphere at its top. If an orifice (opening) exists in the tank at a distance h below the top of the liquid, then the speed of outflow from the orifice is $\sqrt{2gh}$, provided the liquid obeys Bernoulli's equation and the top of the liquid may be regarded as motionless.

Reynolds Number

The **Reynolds number** (N_R) is a dimensionless number that applies to a fluid of viscosity η and density ρ flowing with speed v through a pipe (or past an obstacle) with diameter D:

$$N_R = \frac{\rho v D}{\eta}$$

For systems of the same geometry, flows will usually be similar provided their Reynolds numbers are close. **Turbulent flow** occurs if N_R for the flow exceeds about 2000 for pipes or about 10 for obstacles.

Solved Problems

Solved Problem 2.1 Atmospheric pressure is about 1.01×10^5 Pa. How large a force does the atmosphere exert on a 2 cm^2 area on the top of your head?

Solution. Because p = F/A, where F is perpendicular to A, we have F = pA. Assuming that 2 cm² of your head is flat (nearly correct) and that the force due to the atmosphere is perpendicular to the surface (as it is), we have

$$F = pA = (1.01 \times 10^5 \text{ N/m}^2)(2 \times 10^{-4} \text{ m}^2) = 20 \text{ N}$$

Solved Problem 2.2 The U-tube device connected to the tank in Figure SP2-1 is called a manometer. As you can see, the mercury in the tube stands higher in one side than the other. What is the pressure in the tank if atmospheric pressure is 76 cm of mercury? The density of mercury is 13.6 g/cm³.

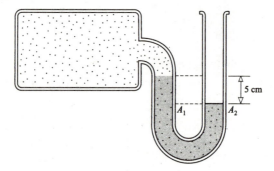

Figure SP2-1

Solution.   Pressure at A_1 = pressure at A_2

(P in tank) + (P due to 5 cm mercury) = (P due to atmosphere)

$$P + (0.05 \text{ m})(13\ 600 \text{ kg/m}^3)(9.8 \text{ m/s}^2)$$
$$= (0.76 \text{ m})(13\ 600 \text{ kg/m}^3)(9.8 \text{ m/s}^2)$$

from which P = 95 kPa.

Or, more simply perhaps, we could note that the pressure in the tank is 5 cm of mercury *lower* than atmospheric. So the pressure is 71 cm of mercury, which is 94.6 kPa.

Chapter 3

HEAT, TEMPERATURE, AND THERMODYNAMICS

IN THIS CHAPTER:

✔ *Thermal Expansion*
✔ *Ideal Gases*
✔ *Heat Quantities*
✔ *Transfer of Heat Energy*
✔ *First Law of Thermodynamics*
✔ *Entropy and the Second Law*
✔ *Solved Problems*

Thermal Expansion

Temperature

Temperature may be measured on the *Celsius* scale, on which the freezing point of water is at 0°C, and the boiling point (under standard conditions) is at 100°C. The *Kelvin* (or absolute) scale is displaced 273.15 Celsius-size degrees from the Celsius scale, so that the freezing point of water is 273.15 K and the boiling point is 373.15 K. Absolute zero is at 0 K (-273.15 °C). The *Fahrenheit* scale is related to the Celsius scale by

$$\text{Fahrenheit temperature} = \frac{9}{5}\left(\text{Celsius temperature}\right) + 32$$

Linear Expansion of Solids

When a solid is subjected to a rise in temperature ΔT, its increase in length ΔL is very nearly proportional to its initial length L_0 multiplied by ΔT, or

$$\Delta L = \alpha L_0 \, \Delta T$$

where the proportionality constant α is called the *coefficient of linear expansion.* The value of α depends on the nature of the substance. From the above equation, α is the change in length per unit length per degree change in temperature. For example, if a 1.000 000 cm length of brass becomes 1.000 019 cm long when the temperature is raised 1.0°C, the linear expansion coefficient for brass is

$$\alpha = \frac{\Delta L}{L_0 \Delta T} = \frac{0.000\ 019\ \text{cm}}{(1.0\ \text{cm})(1.0\ °\text{C})} = 1.9 \times 10^{-5}\ °\text{C}^{-1}$$

Area Expansion

If an area A_0 expands to $A_0 + \Delta A$ when subjected to a temperature rise ΔT, then

$$\Delta A = \gamma A_0 \, \Delta T$$

where γ is the *coefficient of area expansion.* For isotropic solids (those that expand the same way in all directions), $\gamma = 2\alpha$ approximately.

Volume Expansion

If a volume V_0 changes by an amount ΔV when subjected to a temperature change of ΔT, then

$$\Delta V = \beta V_0 \, \Delta T$$

where β is the *coefficient of volume expansion*. This can be either an increase or decrease in volume. For isotropic solids, $\beta = 3\alpha$ approximately.

Ideal Gases

Ideal Gas

An **ideal (or perfect) gas** is one that obeys the Ideal Gas Law, given below. At low to moderate pressures, and at temperatures not too low, the following common gases can be considered ideal: air, nitrogen, oxygen, helium, hydrogen, and neon. Almost any chemically stable gas behaves ideally if it is far removed from conditions under which it will liquefy or solidify. In other words, a real gas behaves like an ideal gas when its atoms or molecules are so far apart that they do not appreciably interact with one another.

One mole of a substance is the amount of the substance that contains as many particles as there are atoms in exactly 12 grams (0.012 kg) of the isotope carbon-12. It follows that one kilomole (kmol) of a substance is the mass (in kg) that is numerically equal to the molecular (or atomic) mass of the substance. For example, the molecular mass of hydrogen gas, H_2, is 2 kg/kmol; hence there are 2 kg in 1 kmol of H_2. Similarly, there are 32 kg in 1 kmol of O_2, and 28 kg in 1 kmol of N_2.

Ideal Gas Law

The absolute pressure P of n kilomoles of gas contained in a volume V is related to the absolute temperature T by

$$PV = nRT$$

where R = 8314 J/kmol • K is called the *universal gas constant*. If the volume contains m kilograms of gas that has a molecular (or atomic) mass M, then n = m/M.

Special cases of the Ideal Gas Law, obtained by holding all but two of its parameters constant, are

Boyle's Law (n, T constant): $PV = $ constant

Charles' Law (n, P constant): $\dfrac{V}{T} = $ constant

Gay–Lussac's Law (n, V constant): $\dfrac{P}{T} = $ constant

Remember
Absolute zero

With n and P constant (Charles' Law), the volume decreases linearly with T and (if the gas remained ideal) would reach zero at T = 0 K. Similarly, with n and V constant (Gay-Lussac's Law), the pressure would decrease to zero with the temperature. This unique temperature at which P and V would reach zero is called **absolute zero**.

Standard Conditions or Standard Temperature and Pressure

Standard conditions or standard temperature and pressure (S.T.P.) are defined to be

T = 273.15 K = 0°C $P = 1.013 \times 10^5$ Pa = 1 atm

Under standard conditions, 1 kmol of ideal gas occupies a volume of 22.4 m^3. Therefore, at S.T.P., 2 kg of H_2 occupies the same volume as 32 kg of O_2 or 28 kg of N_2, namely 22.4 m^3.

Dalton's Law of Partial Pressures

Define the *partial pressure* of one component of a gas mixture to be the pressure the component gas would exert if it alone occupied the entire volume. Then, the total pressure of a mixture of ideal, nonreactive gases is the sum of the partial pressures of the component gases.

Gas Law Problems

Gas law problems involving a change of conditions from (P_1, V_1, T_1) to (P_2, V_2, T_2) are usually easily solved by writing the gas law as

$$\frac{P_1 V_1}{T_1} = \frac{P_2 V_2}{T_2} \quad (\text{at constant } n)$$

Heat Quantities

Thermal Energy

Thermal energy is the random kinetic energy of the particles (usually electrons, ions, atoms, and molecules) composing a system.

Heat

Heat is thermal energy in transit from a system (or aggregate of electrons, ions, and atoms) at one temperature to a system that is in contact with it, but is at a lower temperature. Its SI unit is the joule. Other units used for heat are the calorie (1 cal = 4.184 J) and the British thermal unit (1 Btu = 1054 J). The "Calorie" used by nutritionists is called the "large calorie" and is actually a kilocalorie (1 Cal = 1 kcal = 10^3 cal).

Specific Heat

The **specific heat** (or *specific heat capacity*, c) of a substance is the quantity of heat required to change the temperature of unit mass of the substance by one degree. If a quantity of heat ΔQ is required to produce a temperature change ΔT in a mass m of substance, then the specific heat is

$$c = \frac{\Delta Q}{m\,\Delta T} \text{ or } \Delta Q = cm\,\Delta T$$

In the SI, c has the unit J/kg • K, which is equivalent to J/kg • °C. Also widely used is the unit cal/g • °C, where 1 cal/g • °C = 4184 J/kg • °C.

Each substance has a characteristic value of specific heat, which varies slightly with temperature. For water, c = 4180 J/kg • °C = 1.00 cal/g • °C.

Heat gained (or lost) by a body (whose phase does not change) as it undergoes a temperature change ΔT is given by

$$\Delta Q = mc\,\Delta T$$

The **heat of fusion** (L_f) of a crystalline solid is the quantity of heat required to melt a unit mass of the solid at constant temperature. It is also equal to the quantity of heat given off by a unit mass of the molten solid as it crystallizes at this same temperature. The heat of fusion of water at 0°C is about 335 kJ/kg or 80 cal/g.

The **heat of vaporization** (L_v) of a liquid is the quantity of heat required to vaporize a unit mass of the liquid at constant temperature. For water at 100°C, L_v is about 2.26 MJ/kg or 540 cal/g.

The **heat of sublimation** of a solid substance is the quantity of heat required to convert a unit mass of the substance from the solid to the gaseous state at constant temperature.

Calorimetry Problems

Calorimetry problems involve the sharing of thermal energy among initially hot objects and cold objects. Since energy must be conserved, one can write the following equation:

Sum of heat changes for all objects = 0

Here the heat flowing out of the high-temperature system ($\Delta Q_{out} < 0$) numerically equals the heat flowing into the low-temperature system ($\Delta Q_{out} > 0$) and so the sum is zero. This, of course, assumes that no thermal energy is otherwise lost from the system.

Transfer of Heat Energy

Energy can be transfered by *conduction*, *convection*, and *radiation*. Remember that heat is the energy transferred from a system at a higher temperature to a system at a lower temperature (with which it is in contact) via the collisions of their constituent particles.

Conduction

Conduction occurs when thermal energy moves through a material as a result of collisions between the free electrons, ions, atoms, and molecules of the material. The hotter a substance, the higher the average KE of its atoms. When a temperature difference exists between materials in contact, the higher-energy atoms in the warmer substance transfer energy to the lower-energy atoms in the cooler substance when atomic collisions occur between the two. Heat thus flows from hot to cold.

Consider the slab of material shown in Figure 3-1. Its thickness is L and its cross-sectional area is A. The temperatures of its two faces are T_1 and T_2, so the temperature difference across the slab is $\Delta T = T_1 - T_2$. The quantity $\Delta T/L$ is called the *temperature gradient*. It is the rate-of-change of temperature with distance.

Figure 3-1

The quantity of heat ΔQ transmitted from face 1 to face 2 in time ΔT is given by

$$\frac{\Delta Q}{\Delta t} = k_T A \frac{\Delta T}{L}$$

where k_T depends on the material of the slab and is called the *thermal conductivity* of the material. In the SI, k_T has the unit W/m • K, and $\Delta Q/\Delta t$ is in J/s (i.e., W). Other units sometimes used to express k_T are related to W/m • K as follows:

1 cal/s • cm • °C = 418.4 W/m • K and
1 Btu • in/h • ft^2 • °F = 0.144 W/m • K

Thermal Resistance

The **thermal resistance** (or R value) of a slab is defined by the heat-flow equation in the form

$$\frac{\Delta Q}{\Delta t} = \frac{A\,\Delta T}{R} \quad \text{where } R = \frac{L}{k_T}$$

Its SI unit is m^2 • K/W. Its customary unit is ft^2 • h • °F/Btu, where 1 • ft^2 • h • °F/Btu = 0.176 m^2 • K/W.

For several slabs of the same surface area in series, the combined R value is

$$R = R_1 + R_2 + \cdots + R_N$$

where R_1, $\cdots$, are the R values of the individual slabs.

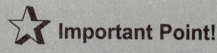

Important Point!

Convection

Convection of thermal energy occurs in a fluid when warm material flows so as to displace cooler material. Typical examples are the flow of warm air from a register in a heating system and the flow of warm water in the Gulf Stream.

Radiation

Radiation is the mode of transport of radiant electromagnetic energy through vacuum and the empty space between atoms. Radiant energy is distinct from heat, though both correspond to energy in transit. Heat is heat; electromagnetic radiation is electromagnetic radiation—don't confuse the two.

A **blackbody** is a body that absorbs all the radiant energy falling on it. At thermal equilibrium, a body emits as much energy as it absorbs. Hence, a good absorber of radiation is also a good emitter of radiation. Suppose a surface of area A has absolute temperature T and radiates only a fraction ε as much energy as would a blackbody surface. Then ε is called the *emissivity* of the surface, and the energy per second (i.e., the power) radiated by the surface is given by the *Stefan-Boltzmann Law*:

$$P = \varepsilon A \sigma T^4$$

where $\sigma = 5.67 \times 10^{-8}$ W/m^2 • K^4 is the *Stefan-Boltzmann constant*, and T is the absolute temperature. The emissivity of a blackbody is unity.

All objects whose temperature is above absolute zero radiate energy. When an object at absolute temperature T is in an environment where the temperature is T_e, the net energy radiated per second by the object is

$$P = \varepsilon A \sigma (T^4 - T_e^4)$$

First Law of Thermodynamics

Heat

Heat (ΔQ) is the thermal energy that flows from one body or system to another, which is in contact with it, because of their temperature difference. Heat always flows from hot to cold. For two objects in contact to be in thermal equilibrium with each other (i.e., for no net heat transfer from one to the other), their temperatures must be the same. If each of two objects is in thermal equilibrium with a third body, then the two are in thermal equilibrium with each other. (This fact is often referred to as the *Zeroth Law of Thermodynamics*.)

Internal Energy

The **internal energy** (U) of a system is the total energy content of the system. It is the sum of all forms of energy possessed by the atoms and molecules of the system.

Work Done by a System

The **work done by a system** (ΔW) is positive if the system thereby loses energy to its surroundings. When the surroundings do work *on* the system so as to give it energy, ΔW is a negative quantity. In a small expansion ΔV, a fluid at constant pressure P does work given by

$$\Delta W = P \, \Delta V$$

First Law of Thermodynamics

The **First Law of Thermodynamics** is a statement of the law of conservation of energy. It states that if an amount of heat (ΔQ) flows into a system, then this energy must appear as increased internal energy ΔU for the system and/or work ΔW done *by* the system on its surroundings. As an equation, the First Law is

$$\Delta Q = \Delta U + \Delta W$$

Thermodynamic Processes

An **isobaric process** is a process carried out at constant pressure.

An **isovolumic process** is a process carried out at constant volume. When a gas undergoes such a process,

$$\Delta W = P \, \Delta V = 0$$

and so the First Law of Thermodynamics becomes

$$\Delta Q = \Delta U$$

Any heat that flows into the system appears as increased internal energy of the system.

An **isothermal process** is a constant-temperature process. In the case of an ideal gas where the constituent atoms or molecules do not interact when separated, $\Delta U = 0$ in an isothermal process. However, this is not true for many other systems. For example, $\Delta U \neq 0$ as ice melts to water at 0°C, even though the process is isothermal.

For an ideal gas, $\Delta U = 0$ is an isothermal change, and so the First Law becomes

$$\Delta Q = \Delta W \qquad \text{(ideal gas)}$$

For an ideal gas changing isothermally from (P_1, V_1) to (P_2, V_2), where $P_1 V_1 = P_2 V_2$,

$$\Delta Q = \Delta W = P_1 V_1 \ln\left(\frac{V_2}{V_1}\right) = 2.30\, P_1 V_1 \log\left(\frac{V_2}{V_1}\right)$$

Here, ln and log are logarithms to the base e and base 10, respectively.

Adiabatic Process

An **adiabatic process** is one in which no heat is transferred to or from the system. For such a process, $\Delta Q = 0$. Hence, in an adiabatic process, the first law becomes

$$0 = \Delta U + \Delta W$$

Any work done by the system is done at the expense of the internal energy. Any work done on the system serves to increase the internal energy.

For an ideal gas changing from conditions (P_1, V_1, T_1) to (P_2, V_2, T_2) in an adiabatic process,

$$P_1 V_1^{\gamma} = P_2 V_2^{\gamma} \quad \text{and} \quad T_1 V_1^{\gamma-1} = T_2 V_2^{\gamma-1}$$

where $\gamma = c_p/c_n$ is discussed below.

Specific Heats of Gases

When a gas is heated *at constant volume*, the heat supplied goes to increase the internal energy of the gas molecules. But when a gas is heated *at constant pressure*, the heat supplied not only increases the internal energy of the molecules but also does mechanical work in expanding the gas against the opposing constant pressure. Hence the specific heat of a gas at constant pressure c_p is greater than its specific heat at constant volume, c_v. It can be shown that, for an ideal gas of molecular mass M,

$$c_p - c_v = \frac{R}{M} \quad (\text{ideal gas})$$

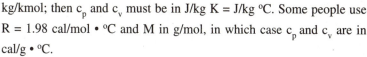

where R is the universal gas constant. In the SI, R = 8314 J/kmol K and M is in kg/kmol; then c_p and c_v must be in J/kg K = J/kg °C. Some people use R = 1.98 cal/mol • °C and M in g/mol, in which case c_p and c_v are in cal/g • °C.

Specific heat ratio ($\gamma = c_p / c_v$): As discussed above, this ratio is greater than unity for a gas. The kinetic theory of gases indicates that for monatomic gases (such as He, Ne, Ar), $\gamma = 1.67$. For diatomic gases (such as O_2, N_2), $\gamma = 1.40$ at ordinary temperatures.

P–V Diagrams

Work is related to area in a P–V diagram. The work done by a fluid in an expansion is equal to the area beneath the expansion curve on a P–V diagram. In a cyclic process, the work output per cycle done by a fluid is equal to the area enclosed by the P–V diagram representing the cycle.

Efficiency of a Heat Engine

The **efficiency of a heat engine** is defined as

$$\text{efficiency} = \frac{\text{work output}}{\text{heat input}}$$

The *Carnot cycle* is the most efficient cycle possible for a heat engine. An engine that operates in accordance to this cycle between a hot reservoir (T_h) and a cold reservoir (T_c) has efficiency

$$\text{efficiency}_{\text{max}} = 1 - \frac{T_c}{T}$$

Kelvin temperatures must be used in this equation.

Entropy and the Second Law

Second Law of Thermodynamics

The **Second Law of Thermodynamics** can be stated in three equivalent ways:

(1) Heat flows spontaneously from a hotter to a colder object, but not vice versa.

(2) No heat engine that cycles continuously can change all its heat-in to useful work-out.

(3) If a system undergoes spontaneous change, it will change in such a way that its entropy will increase or, at best, remain constant.

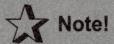 **Note!**

The Second Law tells us the manner in which a spontaneous change will occur, while the First Law tells us whether or not the change is possible. The First Law deals with the conservation of energy; the Second Law deals with the dispersal of energy.

Entropy

Entropy (S) is a *state variable* for a system in equilibrium. By this is meant that S is always the same for the system when it is in a given equilibrium state. Like P, V, and U, the entropy is a characteristic of the system at equilibrium.

When heat ΔQ enters a system at an absolute temperature T, the resulting change in entropy of the system is

$$\Delta S = \frac{\Delta Q}{T}$$

provided the system changes in a reversible way. The SI unit for entropy is J/K.

A *reversible change* (or process) is one in which the values of P, V, T, and U are well defined during the change. If the process is reversed, then P, V, T, and U will take on their original values when the system is returned to where it started. To be reversible, a process must usually be slow, and the system must be close to equilibrium during the entire change.

Another, fully equivalent, definition of entropy can be given from a detailed molecular analysis of the system. If a system can achieve a particular state (i.e., particular values of P, V, T, and U) in Ω (omega) different ways (different arrangements of the molecules, for example), then the entropy of the state is

$$S = k_B \ln \Omega$$

where ln is the logarithm to base e, and k_B is Boltzmann's constant, 1.38×10^{-23} J/K.

Entropy Is a Measure of Disorder

A state that can occur in only one way (one arrangement of its molecules, for example) is a state of high order. But a state that can occur in many ways is a more disordered state. One way to associate a number with disorder is to take the disorder of a state as being proportional to

Ω, the number of ways the state can occur. Because $S = k_B \ln \Omega$, entropy is a measure of disorder.

Spontaneous processes in systems that contain many molecules always occur in a direction from a

$$\begin{pmatrix} \text{state that can exist} \\ \text{in only a few ways} \end{pmatrix} \rightarrow \begin{pmatrix} \text{state that can exist} \\ \text{in many ways} \end{pmatrix}$$

Hence, when left to themselves, systems retain their original state of order or else increase their disorder.

The most probable state of a system is the state with the largest entropy. It is also the state with the most disorder and the state that can occur in the largest number of ways.

Solved Problems

Solved Problem 3.1 A 20 g piece of aluminum ($c = 0.21$ cal/g °C) at 90 °C is dropped into a cavity in a large block of ice at 0 °C. How much ice does the aluminum melt?

Solution.

(heat change of Al as it cools to 0 °C)
$$+ \text{(heat change of mass m of ice melted)} = 0$$

$$(m \ c \ \Delta T)_{Al} + (H_f m)_{ice} = 0$$

$$(20 \text{ g})(0.21 \text{ cal/g °C})(0 \text{ °C} - 90 \text{ °C}) + (80 \text{ cal/g}) \ m = 0$$

from which $m = 4.7$ g is the quantity of ice melted.

Solved Problem 3.2 What is the net work output per cycle for the thermodynamic cycle in Figure SP3-1?

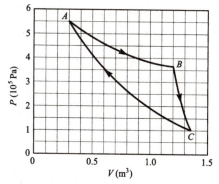

Figure SP3-1

Solution. We know that the net work output per cycle is the area enclosed by the P-V diagram. We estimate that in area ABCA there are 22 squares, each of area

$$(0.5 \times 10^5 \text{ N/m}^2)(0.1 \text{ m}^3) = 5 \text{ kJ}$$

Therefore,

Area enclosed by cycle $\approx$ (22)(5 kJ) = 110 kJ

Chapter 4
WAVES

IN THIS CHAPTER:

✔ *Transverse Waves*
✔ *Wave Terminology*
✔ *Standing Waves*
✔ *Resonance*
✔ *Longitudinal Waves*
✔ *Sound Waves*
✔ *Doppler Effect*

Transverse Waves

Propagating Waves

A **propagating wave** is a self-sustaining disturbance of a medium that travels from one point to another, carrying energy and momentum. Mechanical waves are aggregate phenomena arising from the motion of constituent particles. The wave advances, but the particles of the medium only oscillate in place. A wave has been generated on the string in Figure 4-1 by the sinusoidal vibration of the hand at its end. The wave furnishes a record of earlier vibrations of the source. Energy is carried by the wave from the source to the right, along the string. This direction, the direction of energy transport, is called the direction (or line) of propagation of the wave.

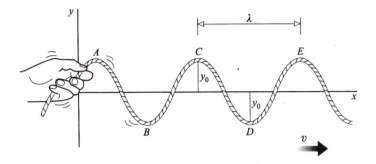

Figure 4-1

Each particle of the string (such as the one at point C) vibrates up and down, perpendicular to the line of propagation. Any wave in which the vibration direction is perpendicular to the direction of propagation is called a *transverse wave*. Typical transverse waves, besides those on a string, are electromagnetic waves—light and radio waves. By contrast, in sound waves, the vibration direction is parallel to the direction of propagation, as will be seen in a later section. Such a wave is called a *longitudinal* (or *compressional*) *wave*.

Wave Terminology

The **period** (T) of a wave is the time it takes the wave to go through one complete cycle. It is the time taken for a particle such as the one at A to move through one complete vibration or cycle, down from point A and then back to A. The period is the number of seconds per cycle. The **frequency** (f) of a wave is the number of cycles per second. Thus,

$$f = \frac{1}{T}$$

If T is in seconds, then f is in hertz (Hz), where $1 \text{ Hz} = 1 \text{ s}^{-1}$. The period and frequency of the wave are the same as the period and frequency of the vibration

The top points on the wave, such as A and C, are called *wave crests*. The bottom points, such as B and D, are called *troughs*. As time goes on, the crests and troughs move to the right with speed v, the speed of the wave. The **amplitude** of a wave is the maximum disturbance undergone during a vibration cycle, distance y_0 in Figure 4-1. The **wavelength** (λ) is the distance along the direction of propagation between corresponding points on the wave, distance AC, for example. In a time T, a crest moving with speed v will move a distance λ to the right. Therefore, s = vt gives

$$\lambda = vT = \frac{v}{f} \quad \text{and} \quad v = f\lambda$$

This relation holds for all waves, not just for waves on a string.

In-phase vibrations exist at two points on a wave if those points undergo vibrations that are in the same direction, in step. For example, the particles of the string at points A and C in Figure 4-1 vibrate in-phase, since they move up together and down together. Vibrations are in-phase if the points are a whole number of wavelengths apart. The pieces of the string at A and B vibrate opposite to each other; the vibrations there are said to be $180°$, or half a cycle, *out-of-phase*.

The **speed of a transverse wave** on a stretched string or wire is

$$v = \sqrt{\frac{\text{tension in string}}{\text{mass per unit length of string}}}$$

Standing Waves

At certain vibrational frequencies, a system can undergo resonance. That is to say, it can efficiently absorb energy from a driving source in its environment which is oscillating at that frequency (see Figure 4-2).

These and similar vibration patterns are called **standing waves**, as compared to the propagating waves considered above. These might better not be called waves at all since they do not transport energy and momentum. The stationary points (such as B and D) are called **nodes**; the points of greatest motion (such as A, C, and E) are called **antinodes**.

The distance between adjacent nodes (or antinodes) is $\frac{1}{2}\lambda$.

We term the portion of the string between adjacent nodes a **segment**, and the length of a segment is also $\frac{1}{2}\lambda$.

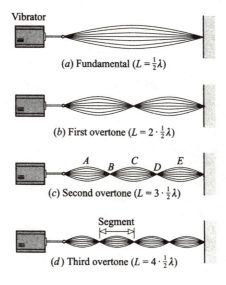

(a) Fundamental $(L = \frac{1}{2}\lambda)$

(b) First overtone $(L = 2 \cdot \frac{1}{2}\lambda)$

(c) Second overtone $(L = 3 \cdot \frac{1}{2}\lambda)$

(d) Third overtone $(L = 4 \cdot \frac{1}{2}\lambda)$

Figure 4-2

Resonance

A string will resonate only if the vibration wavelength has certain special values: the wavelength must be such that a whole number of wave segments (each $\frac{1}{2}\lambda$ long) exactly fit on the string. A proper fit occurs when nodes and antinodes exist at positions demanded by the constraints on the string. In particular, the fixed ends of the string must be nodes. Thus, as shown in Figure 4-2, the relation between the wavelength λ and the length L of the resonating string is $L = n\left(\frac{1}{2}\lambda\right)$, where n is any integer. Because $\lambda = vT = v/f$, the shorter the wave segments at resonance, the higher will be the resonance frequency. If we call the fundamental resonance frequency f_1, then Figure 4-2 shows that the higher resonance frequencies are given by $f_n = nf_1$.

Longitudinal Waves

Longitudinal (compressional) waves occur as lengthwise vibrations of air columns, solid bars, and the like. At resonance, nodes exist at fixed points, such as the closed end of an air column in a tube, or the location of a clamp on a bar. Diagrams such as Figure 4-2 are used to display the resonance of longitudinal waves as well as transverse waves. However, for longitudinal waves, the diagrams are mainly schematic and are used simply to indicate the locations of nodes and antinodes. In analyzing such diagrams, we use the fact that the distance between node and adjacent antinode is $\frac{1}{4}\lambda$.

Sound Waves

Sound waves are compression waves in a material medium such as air, water, or steel. When the compressions and rarefactions of the waves strike the eardrum, they result in the sensation of sound, provided the frequency of the waves is between about 20 Hz and 20 000 Hz. Waves with frequencies above 20 kHz

are called *ultrasonic* waves. Those with frequencies below 20 Hz are called *infrasonic* waves.

Equations for Sound Speed

In an ideal gas of molecular mass M and absolute temperature T, the speed of sound v is given by

$$v = \sqrt{\frac{\gamma RT}{M}} \quad \text{(ideal gas)}$$

where R is the gas constant, and γ is the ratio of specific heats c_p/c_v. γ is about 1.67 for monatomic gases (He, Ne, Ar), and about 1.40 for diatomic gases (N_2, O_2, H_2).

The speed of compression waves in other materials is given by

$$v = \sqrt{\frac{\text{modulus}}{\text{density}}}$$

If the material is in the form of a bar, Young's modulus Y is used. For liquids, one must use the bulk modulus.

The **speed of sound in air** at 0°C is 331 m/s. The speed increases with temperature by about 0.61 m/s for each 1°C rise. More precisely, sound speeds v_1 and v_2 at absolute temperatures T_1 and T_2 are related by

$$\frac{v_1}{v_2} = \sqrt{\frac{T_1}{T_2}}$$

The speed of sound is essentially independent of pressure, frequency, and wavelength.

Intensity

The **intensity** (I) of any wave is the energy per unit area, per unit time; in practice, it is the average power carried by the wave through a unit area erected perpendicular to the direction of propagation of the wave. Suppose that in a time Δt an amount of energy ΔE is carried through an area ΔA that is perpendicular to the propagation direction of the wave. Then

$$I = \frac{\Delta E}{\Delta A\, \Delta t} = \frac{P_{av}}{\Delta A}$$

It may be shown that, for a sound wave with amplitude A_0 and frequency f, traveling with speed v in a material of density ρ,

$$I = 2\pi^2 f^2 \rho v A_0^2$$

If f is in Hz, ρ is in kg/m^3, v is in m/s, and A_0 (the maximum displacement of the atoms or molecules of the medium) is in m, then I is in W/m^2.

Loudness

Loudness is a measure of the human perception of sound. Although a sound wave of high intensity is perceived as louder than a wave of lower intensity, the relation is far from linear. The sensation of sound is roughly proportional to the logarithm of the sound intensity. But the exact relation between loudness and intensity is complicated and not the same for all individuals.

Intensity (or loudness) level (β) is defined by an arbitrary scale that corresponds roughly to the sensation of loudness. The zero on this scale is taken at the sound-wave intensity $I_0 = 1.00 \times 10^{-12}$ W/m^2, which corresponds roughly to the weakest audible sound. The intensity level, in decibels, is then defined by

$$\beta = 10 \, \log\left(\frac{I}{I_o}\right)$$

The *decibel* (dB) is a dimensionless unit. The normal ear can distinguish between intensities that differ by an amount down to about 1 dB.

Remember!

Beats

The alternations of maximum and minimum intesity produced by the superposition of two waves of slightly different frequencies are called *beats*. The number of beats per second is equal to the difference between the frequencies of the two waves that are combined.

Doppler Effect

Suppose that a moving sound source emits a sound of frequency f_s. Let v be the speed of sound, and let the source approach the listener or observer at speed v_s, measured relative to the medium conducting the sound. Suppose further that the observer is moving toward the source at speed v_o, also measured relative to the medium. Then the observer will hear a sound of frequency f_o given by

$$f_o = f_s\left(\frac{v + v_o}{v - v_s}\right)$$

If either the source or the observer is moving away from the other, the sign on its speed in the equation must be changed.

When the source and the observer are approaching each other, more wave crests strike the ear each second than when both are at rest. This causes the ear to perceive a higher frequency than that emitted by the source. When the two are receding, the opposite effect occurs; the frequency appears to be lowered.

Because $v + v_o$ is the speed of a wave crest relative to the observer, and because $v - v_s$ is the speed of a wave crest relative to the source, an alternative form is

$$f_o = f_s \left(\frac{\text{crest speed relative to observer}}{\text{crest speed relative to source}} \right)$$

Interference Effects

Two sound waves of the same frequency and amplitude may give rise to easily observed interference effects at a point through which they both pass. If the crests of one wave fall on the crests of the other, the two waves are said to be *in-phase*. In that case, they reinforce each other and give rise to a high intensity at that point.

However, if the crests of one wave fall on the troughs of the other, the two waves will exactly cancel each other. No sound will then be heard at the point. We say that the two waves are then 180° (or a half wavelength) *out-of-phase*.

Intermediate effects are observed if the two waves are neither in-phase nor 180° out-of-phase, but have a fixed phase relationship somewhere in between.

Chapter 5

ELECTRICITY AND MAGNETISM

IN THIS CHAPTER:

- ✔ Coulomb's Law and Electric Fields
- ✔ Potential and Capacitance
- ✔ Current, Resistance, and Ohm's Law
- ✔ Electrical Power
- ✔ Equivalent Resistance, Simple Circuits, and Kirchhoff's Laws
- ✔ Magnetic Fields
- ✔ Induced EMF and Magnetic Flux
- ✔ Electric Generators and Motors
- ✔ Inductance; R-C and R-L Time Constants
- ✔ Alternating Current
- ✔ Solved Problems

Coulomb's Law and Electric Fields

Coulomb's Law

Suppose that two point charges, q and q´, are a distance r apart in vacuum. If q and q´ have the same sign, the two charges repel each other; if they have opposite signs, they attract each other. The force experienced by either charge due to the other is called a **Coulomb** or **electric force,** and it is given by **Coulomb's law,**

$$F_E = k\frac{qq'}{r^2} \quad (\text{in vacuum})$$

As always in the SI, distances are measured in meters and forces in newtons. The SI unit for charge q is the *coulomb* (C). The constant k in Coulomb's Law has the value

$k = 8.988 \times 10^9$ N • m^2/C^2

which we shall usually approximate as 9.0×10^9 N • m^2/C^2. Often, k is replaced by $1/4\pi\varepsilon_0$, where $\varepsilon_0 = 8.85 \times 10^{-12}$ C^2/N • m^2 is called the *permittivity of free space*. Then Coulomb's Law becomes

$$F_E = \frac{1}{4\pi\varepsilon_0}\frac{qq'}{r^2} \quad (\text{in vacuum})$$

When the surrounding medium is not a vacuum, forces caused by induced charges in the material reduce the force between point charges. If the material has a *dielectric constant* K, then ε_0 in Coulomb's Law must be replaced by $K\varepsilon_0 = \varepsilon$, where ε is called the *permittivity of the material*. Then,

$$F_E = \frac{1}{4\pi\varepsilon}\frac{qq'}{r^2} = \frac{k}{K}\frac{qq'}{r^2}$$

For vacuum, $K = 1$; for air, $K = 1.0006$.

Coulomb's Law also applies to uniform spherical shells or spheres of charge. In that case, r, the distance between the centers of the spheres, must be larger than the sum of the radii of the spheres.

Charge Is Quantized

The magnitude of the smallest charge ever measured is denoted by e (called the quantum of charge), where $e = 1.602\ 18 \times 10^{-19}$ C. All free charges, ones that can be isolated and measured, are integer multiples of e. The electron has a charge of -e, while the proton's charge is +e.

Conservation of Charge

The algebraic sum of the charges in the isolated system is constant. When a particle with charge +e is created, a particle with charge -e is simultaneously created in the immediate vicinity. When a particle with charge +e disappears, a particle with charge -e also disappears in the immediate vicinity. Hence, the net charge of the isolated system remains constant.

The Test-Charge Concept

A *test-charge* is a very small charge that can be used in making measurements on an electric system. It is assumed that such a charge, which is tiny both in magnitude and in physical size, has a negligible effect on its environment.

Electric Field

An **electric field** is said to exist at any point in space when a test charge, placed at that point, experiences an electrical force. The direction of the electric field at a point is the same as the direction of the force experienced by a *positive* test charge placed at the point.

Electric field lines can be used to sketch electric fields. The line through a point has the same direction at that point as the electric field. Where the field lines are closest together, the electric field is largest. Field lines come out of positive charges (because a positive charge repels a positive test charge) and come into negative charges (because they attract the positive test charge).

The **strength of the electric field** ($\vec{E}$) at a point is equal to the force experienced by a unit positive test charge placed at that point. Because the electric field strength is a force per unit charge, it is a vector quantity. The units of $\vec{E}$ are N/C or V/m (as will be shown later). If a charge q is placed at a point where the electric field due to other charges is $\vec{E}$, the charge will experience a force $\vec{F}_E$ is given by

$$\vec{F}_E = q\vec{E}$$

If q is negative, $\vec{F}_E$, will be opposite in direction to $\vec{E}$.

Electric Field Due to a Point Charge

To find E (the signed magnitude of $\vec{E}$) due to a point charge q, we make use of Coulomb's Law. If a point charge q´ is placed at a distance r from the charge q, it will experience a force

$$F_E = \frac{1}{4\pi\varepsilon}\frac{qq'}{r^2} = q'\left(\frac{1}{4\pi\varepsilon}\frac{q}{r^2}\right)$$

But if a point charge q′ is placed at a position where the electric field is E, then the force on q′ is

$$F_E = q'\,E$$

Comparing these two expressions for F_E, we see that

$$E = \frac{1}{4\pi\varepsilon}\frac{q}{r^2}$$

This is the electric field at a distance r from a point charge q. The same relation applies at points outside a finite spherical charge q. For q positive, E is positive and $\vec{E}$ is directed radially outward from q; for q negative, E is negative and $\vec{E}$ is directed radially inward.

Superposition Principle

The force experienced by a charge due to other charges is the vector sum of the Coulomb forces acting on it due to these other charges.

Similarly, the electric intensity $\vec{E}$ at a point due to several charges is the vector sum of the intensities due to the individual charges.

Potential and Capacitance

Potential Difference

The **potential difference** between point A and point B is the work done against electrical forces in carrying a unit positive test-charge from A to B. We represent the potential difference between A and B by $V_B - V_A$ or by V. Its units are those of work per charge (joules/coulomb) and are called *volts* (V):

$$1 V = 1 J/C$$

Because work is a scalar quantity, so too is potential difference. Like work, potential difference may be positive or negative. The work W done in transporting a charge q from one point A to a second point B is

$$W = q(V_B - V_A) = qV$$

where the appropriate sign (+ or -) must be given to the charge. If both $(V_B - V_A)$ and q are positive (or negative), the work done is positive. If $(V_B - V_A)$ and q have opposite signs, the work done is negative.

Absolute Potential

The absolute potential at a point is the work done against electric forces in carrying a unit positive test-charge from infinity to that point. Hence the absolute potential at a point B is the difference in potential from A $= \infty$ to B.

Consider a point charge q in vacuum and a point P at a distance r from the point charge. The absolute potential at P due to the charge q is

$$V = k\frac{q}{r}$$

where $k = 8.99 \times 10^9$ N • m^2/C^2 is the Coulomb constant. The absolute potential at infinity (at $r = \infty$) is zero.

Because of the superposition principle and the scalar nature of potential difference, the absolute potential at a point due to a number of point charges is

$$V = k \sum \frac{q_i}{r_i}$$

where the r_i are the distances of the charges q_i from the point in question. Negative q's contribute negative terms to the potential, while positive q's contribute positive terms.

The absolute potential due to a uniformly charged sphere, at points outside the sphere or on its surface, is

$$V = k \frac{q}{r}$$

where q is the charge on the sphere. This potential is the same as that due to a point charge q placed at the position of the sphere's center.

Electrical Potential Energy

To carry a charge q from infinity to a point where the absolute potential is V, work in the amount qV must be done on the charge. This work appears as **electrical potential energy** (EPE) stored in the charge.

Similarly, when a charge q is carried through a potential difference V, work in the amount qV must be done on the charge. This work results in a change qV in the EPE of the charge. For a potential rise, V will be positive and the EPE will increase if q is positive. But for a potential drop, V will be negative and the EPE of the charge will decrease if q is positive.

Suppose that in a certain region the electric field is uniform and is in the x-direction. Call its magnitude E_x. Because E_x is the force on a unit positive test-charge, the work done in moving the test-charge through a distance x is (from $W = F_x x$)

$$V = E_x x$$

The field between two large, parallel, oppositely charged metal plates is uniform. We can therefore use this equation to relate the electric field E between the plates to the plate separation d and their potential difference V:

$$V = Ed$$

The work done in carrying a charge +e (coulombs) through a potential rise of exactly 1 volt is defined to be 1 electron volt (eV). Therefore,

$$1 \text{ eV} = (1.602 \ 10^{-19} \text{ C})(1 \text{ V}) = 1.602 \times 10^{-19} \text{ J}$$

Equivalently,

$$\text{Work or energy (in eV)} = \frac{\text{work (in joules)}}{e}$$

Capacitors

A **capacitor** is a device that stores charge. Often, although certainly not always, it consists of two conductors separated by an insulator or dielectric. The *capacitance* (C) of a capacitor is defined as

$$\text{Capacitance} = \frac{\text{magnitude of charge on either conductor}}{\text{magnitude of potential difference between conductors}}$$

For q in coulombs and V in volts, C is in farads (F).

The capacitance of a **parallel-plate capacitor** whose opposing plate faces, each of area A, are separated by a small distance d is given by

$$C = K\varepsilon_0 \frac{A}{d}$$

where $K = \varepsilon/\varepsilon_0$ is the dimensionless dielectric constant of the noncon-ducting material (the *dielectric*) between the plates, and

$$\varepsilon_0 = 8.85 \times 10^{-12} \ C^2/N \cdot m^2 = 8.85 \times 10^{-12} \ F/m$$

For vacuum, $K = 1$, so that a dielectric-filled parallel-plate capacitor has a capacitance K times larger than the same capacitor with vacuum between its plates. This result holds for a capacitor of arbitrary shape.

As shown in Figure 5-1, capacitances add for capacitors in parallel, whereas reciprocal capacitances add for capacitors in series.

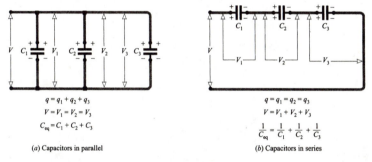

$$q = q_1 + q_2 + q_3$$
$$V = V_1 = V_2 = V_3$$
$$C_{eq} = C_1 + C_2 + C_3$$

(*a*) Capacitors in parallel

$$q = q_1 = q_2 = q_3$$
$$V = V_1 + V_2 + V_3$$
$$\frac{1}{C_{eq}} = \frac{1}{C_1} + \frac{1}{C_2} + \frac{1}{C_3}$$

(*b*) Capacitors in series

Figure 5-1

Energy Stored in a Capacitor

The energy EPE stored in a capacitor of capacitance C that has a charge q and a potential difference V is

$$EPE = \frac{1}{2} qV = \frac{1}{2} CV^2 = \frac{1}{2} \frac{q^2}{C}$$

Current, Resistance, and Ohm's Law

Current

A **current** (I) of electricity exists in a region when a net electric charge is transported from one point to another in that region. Suppose the charge is moving through a wire. If a charge q is transported through a given cross section of the wire in a time t, then the current through the wire is

$$I = \frac{q}{t}$$

Here q is in coulombs, t is in seconds, and I is in amperes (1 A = 1 C/s). By custom, the direction of the current is taken to be in the direction of flow of positive charge. Thus, a flow of electrons to the right corresponds to a current to the left.

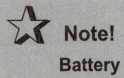

Note!

Battery

A **battery** is a source of electrical energy. If no internal energy losses occur in the battery, then the potential difference between its terminals is called the *electromotive force* (emf) of the battery. Unless otherwise stated, it will be assumed that the terminal potential difference of a battery is equal to its emf. The unit for emf is the same as the unit for potential difference, the volt.

Resistance

The **resistance** (R) of a wire or other object is a measure of the potential difference (V) that must be impressed across the object to cause a current of one ampere to flow through it:

$$R = \frac{V}{I}$$

The unit of resistance is the *ohm*, for which the symbol Ω (greek omega) is used. $1 \Omega = 1$ V/A.

Ohm's Law

Ohm's Law originally contained two parts. Its first part was simply the defining equation for resistance, V = IR. We often refer to this equation as being Ohm's Law. However, Ohm also stated that R is a constant independent of V and I. This latter part of the Law is only approximately correct. The relation V = IR can be applied to any resistor, where V is the potential difference (p.d.) between the two ends of the resistor, I is the current through the resistor, and R is the resistance of the resistor under those conditions.

Terminal Potential Difference

The **terminal potential difference** (or voltage) of a battery or generator when it delivers a current I is related to its electromotive force $\mathscr{E}$ and its *internal resistance* r as follows:

(1)   When delivering current (on discharge):

Terminal voltage = (emf) - (voltage drop in internal resistance)

$$V = \mathscr{E} - Ir$$

(2)   When receiving current (on charge):

Terminal voltage = (emf) + (voltage drop in internal resistance)

$$V = \mathscr{E} + Ir$$

(3)   When no current exists:

Terminal voltage = emf of battery or generator

Resistivity

The resistance R of a wire of length L and cross-sectional area A is

$$R = \rho \frac{L}{A}$$

where ρ is a constant called the *resistivity*. The resistivity is a characteristic of the material from which the wire is made. For L in m, A in m^2, and R in Ω, the units of ρ are $\Omega \cdot m$.

Resistance Varies With Temperature

If a wire has a resistance R_0 at a temperature T_0, then its resistance R at a temperature T is

$$R = R_o + \alpha R_o (T - T_o)$$

where α is the *temperature coefficient of resistance* of the material of the wire. Usually, α varies with temperature, and so this relation is applicable only over a small temperature range. The units of α are K^{-1} or $°C^{-1}$.

A similar relation applies to the variation of resistivity with temperature. If ρ_0 and ρ are the resistivities at T_0 and T, respectively, then

$$\rho = \rho_o + \alpha \rho_o (T - T_o)$$

Potential Changes

The potential difference across a resistor R through which a current I flows is, by Ohm's Law, IR. The end of the resistor at which the current enters is the high-potential end of the resistor. Current always flows "downhill," from high to low potential, through a resistor. The positive terminal of a battery is always the high-potential terminal if the internal resistance of the battery is negligible or small. This is true irrespective of the direction of the current through the battery.

Electrical Power

Electrical Work

The **electrical work** (in joules) required to transfer a charge q (in coulombs) through a potential difference V (in volts) is given by

$$W = qV$$

When q and V are given their proper signs (i.e., voltage rises positive and drops negative), the work will have its proper sign. Thus, to carry a positive charge through a potential rise, a positive amount of work must be done on the charge.

Electrical Power

The **electrical power** (in watts) delivered by an energy source as it carries a charge q (in coulombs) through a potential rise V (in volts) in a time t (in seconds) is

$$\text{Power} = \frac{\text{work}}{\text{time}}$$

$$P = \frac{Vq}{t}$$

Because q/t = I, this can be rewritten as

$$P = VI$$

where I is in amperes.

The **power loss in a resistor** is found by replacing V in VI by IR, or by replacing I in VI by V/R, to obtain

$$P = VI = I^2R = \frac{V^2}{R}$$

The **thermal energy generated in a resistor** per second is equal to the power loss in the resistor:

$$P = VI = I^2R$$

You Need to Know ✔

Convenient Conversions

1 W = 1 J/s = 0.239 cal/s = 0.738 ft · lb/s
1 kW = 1.341 hp = 56.9 Btu/min
1 hp = 746 W = 33 000 ft · lb/min = 42.4 Btu/min
1 kW · h = 3.6×10^6 J = 3.6 MJ

Equivalent Resistance, Simple Circuits, and Kirchhoff's Laws

Resistors in Series

When current can follow only one path as it flows through two or more resistors connected in line, the resistors are in *series*. In other words, when one and only one terminal of a resistor is connected directly to one and only one terminal of another resistor, the two are in series and the same current passes through both. A *node* is a point where three or more current-carrying wires or branches meet. There are no nodes between circuit elements (such as capacitors, resistors, and batteries) that are connected in series. A typical case is shown in Figure 5-2(a).

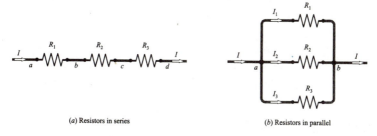

(a) Resistors in series   (b) Resistors in parallel

Figure 5-2

For several resistors in series, their equivalent resistance R_{eq} is given by

$$R_{eq} = R_1 + R_2 + R_3 + \cdots \quad \text{(series combination)}$$

where R_1, R_2, R_3, . . ., are the resistances of the several resistors. Observe that resistances in series combine like capacitances in parallel. It is assumed that all connection wire is effectively resistanceless.

In a series combination, the current through each resistance is the same as that through all the others. The potential drop (p.d.) across the combination is equal to the sum of the individual potential drops. The equivalent resistance in series is always greater than the largest of the individual resistances.

Resistors in Parallel

Several resistors are connected in parallel between two nodes if one end of each resistor is connected to one node and the other end of each is connected to the other node. A typical case is shown in Figure 5-2(b), where points a and b are nodes. Their equivalent resistance R_{eq} is given by

$$\frac{1}{R_{eq}} = \frac{1}{R_1} + \frac{1}{R_2} + \frac{1}{R_3} + \cdots \text{(parallel combination)}$$

The equivalent resistance in parallel is always less than the smallest of the individual resistances. Connecting additional resistances in parallel decreases R_{eq} for the combination. Observe that resistances in parallel combine like capacitances in series.

The potential drop V across each resistor in a parallel combination is the same as the potential drop across each of the others. The current through the nth resistor is $I_n = V/R_n$ and the total current entering the combination is equal to the sum of the individual branch currents.

Kirchhoff's Laws

Kirchhoff's node (or junction) rule
The sum of all the currents coming into a node (i.e., a junction where three or more current-carrying leads attach) must equal the sum of all the currents leaving that node.

Kirchhoff's loop (or circuit) rule
As one traces out a closed circuit, the algebraic sum of the potential changes encountered is zero. In this sum, a potential rise is positive and a potential drop is negative. Current always flows from high to low potential through a resistor. As one traces through a resistor in the direction of the current, the potential change is negative because it is a potential drop. The positive terminal of a pure emf source is always the high-potential terminal, independent of the direction of the current through the emf source.

The set of equations obtained by use of Kirchhoff's loop rule will be independent provided that each new loop equation contains a voltage change not included in a previous equation.

Magnetic Fields

Magnetic Field

A **magnetic field** $\left(\vec{B} \right)$ exists in an otherwise empty region of space if a charge moving through that region can experience a force due to its motion (as shown in Figure 5-3). Frequently, a magnetic field is detected by its effect on a compass needle (a tiny bar magnet). The compass needle lines up in the direction of the magnetic field.

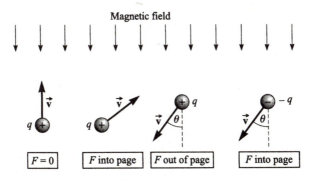

Figure 5-3

Magnetic Field Lines

Magnetic field lines drawn in a region provide a means for showing the direction in which a compass needle placed in the region will point. A method for determining the field lines near a bar magnet is shown in Figure 5-4. By tradition, we take the direction of the compass needle to be the direction of the field.

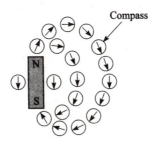

Figure 5-4

Magnet

A **magnet** may have two or more poles, although it must have at least one *north pole* and one *south pole*. Because a compass needle points away from a north pole (N in Figure 5-4) and toward a south pole (S), magnetic field lines exit north poles and enter south poles.

Magnetic poles of the same type (north or south) repel each other, while unlike poles attract each other.

Charge Moving through a Magnetic Field

A charge moving through a magnetic field experiences a force due to the field, provided its velocity vector is not along a magnetic field line.

In Figure 5-3, charges (q) are moving with velocity $\vec{v}$ in a magnetic field directed as shown. The direction of the force $\vec{F}$ on each charge is indicated. Notice that the direction of the force on a negative charge is opposite to that on a positive charge with the same velocity.

The direction of the force acting on a charge +q moving in a magnetic field can be found from a *right-hand rule* (Figure 5-5):

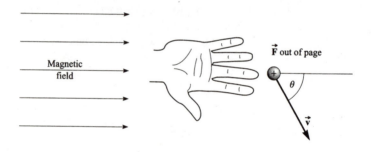

Figure 5-5

Hold the right hand flat. Point its fingers in the direction of the field. Orient the thumb along the direction of the velocity of the positive charge. Then the palm of the hand pushes in the direction of the force on the charge. The force direction on a negative charge is opposite to that on a positive charge.

It is often helpful to note that the field line through the particle and the velocity vector of the particle determine a plane (the plane of the page in Figure 5-5). The force vector is always perpendicular to this plane.

The **magnitude of the force** (F) on a charge moving in a magnetic field depends upon the product of four factors:

(1) q, the charge (in C)
(2) v, the magnitude of the velocity of the charge (in m/s)
(3) B, the strength of the magnetic field
(4) sin θ, where θ is the angle between the field lines and the velocity $\vec{v}$.

The **magnetic field at a point** is represented by a vector $\vec{B}$ that is variously called the *magnetic induction*, the *magnetic flux density*, or simply the *magnetic field*.

We define the magnitude of $\vec{B}$ and its units by way of the equation

$$F_M = qvB \sin \theta$$

where F_M is in newtons, q is in coulombs, v is in m/s, and B is the magnetic field in a unit called the *tesla* (T). A tesla can also be expressed as a *weber per square meter*: $1 \text{ T} = 1 \text{ Wb/m}^2$.

Still encountered is the cgs unit for B, the *gauss* (G), where

$$1 \text{ G} = 10^{-4} \text{ T}$$

The Earth's magnetic field is a few tenths of a gauss. Also note that

$$1 \text{ T} = 1 \text{ Wb/m}^2 = 1 \ \frac{N}{C \ (m/s)} = 1 \ \frac{N}{A \ m}$$

Force on a Current in a Magnetic Field

Since current is simply a stream of positive charges, a current experiences a force due to a magnetic field. The direction of the force is found by the right-hand rule shown in Figure 5-5, with the direction of the current used in place of the velocity vector.

The magnitude ΔF_M of the force on a small length ΔL of wire carrying current I is given by

$$\Delta F_M = I(\Delta L)B \sin \theta$$

where θ is the angle between the direction of the current I and the direction of the field. For a straight wire of length L in a uniform magnetic field, this becomes

$$F_M = I L B \sin \theta$$

Notice that the force is zero if the wire is in line with the field lines. The force is maximum if the field lines are perpendicular to the wire. In analogy to the case of a moving charge, the force is perpendicular to the plane defined by the wire and the field lines.

Torque on a Flat Coil

The torque τ on a coil of N loops, each carrying a current I, in an external magnetic field B is

$$\tau = NIAB \sin \theta$$

where A is the area of the coil, and θ is the angle between the field lines and a perpendicular to the plane of the coil. For the direction of rotation of the coil, we have the following right-hand rule:

> Orient the right thumb perpendicular to the plane of the coil, such that the fingers run in the direction of the current flow. Then the torque acts to rotate the thumb into alignment with the external field (at which orientation the torque will be zero).

Sources of Magnetic Fields

Magnetic fields are produced by moving charges, and of course that includes electric currents. Figure 5-6 shows the nature of the magnetic fields produced by several current configurations. Below each is given the value of B at the indicated point P. The constant $\mu_0 = 4\pi \times 10^{-7}$ T • m/A is called the *permeability of free space*. It is assumed that the surrounding material is vacuum or air.

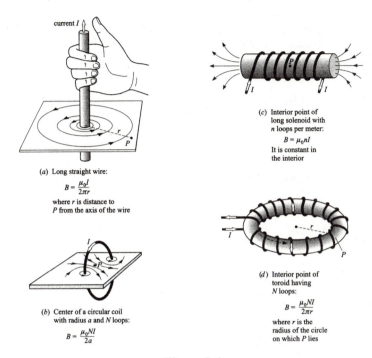

(a) Long straight wire:

$$B = \frac{\mu_0 I}{2\pi r}$$

where r is distance to
P from the axis of the wire

(b) Center of a circular coil
with radius a and N loops:

$$B = \frac{\mu_0 NI}{2a}$$

(c) Interior point of
long solenoid with
n loops per meter:

$$B = \mu_0 nI$$

It is constant in
the interior

(d) Interior point of
toroid having
N loops:

$$B = \frac{\mu_0 NI}{2\pi r}$$

where r is the
radius of the circle
on which P lies

Figure 5-6

The direction of the magnetic field of a current-carrying wire can be found by using a right-hand rule, as illustrated in Figure 5-6(a):

> Grasp the wire in the right hand, with the thumb pointing in the direction of the current. The fingers then circle the wire in the same direction as the magnetic field does.

This same rule can be used to find the direction of the field for a current loop such as that shown in Figure 5-6(b).

Ferromagnetic Materials

Ferromagnetic materials, primarily iron and the other transition elements, greatly enhance magnetic fields. The ferromagnetic materials contain *domains*, or regions of aligned atoms, that act as tiny bar magnets. When the domains within an object are aligned with each other, the object becomes a magnet. The alignment of domains in permanent magnets is not easily disrupted.

Magnetic Moment

The **magnetic moment** of a flat current-carrying loop (current = I, area = A) is IA. The magnetic moment is a vector quantity that points along the field line perpendicular to the plane of the loop. In terms of the magnetic moment, the torque on a flat coil with N loops in a magnetic field B is

$$\tau = N(IA)B \sin \theta$$

where θ is the angle between the field and the magnetic moment vector.

Magnetic Field of a Current Element

The current element of length ΔL shown in Figure 5-7 contributes $\Delta \vec{B}$ to the field at P. The magnitude of $\Delta \vec{B}$ is given by the *Biot–Savart Law*:

$$\Delta B = \frac{\mu_o I \Delta L}{4\pi r^2} \sin \theta$$

where r and θ are defined in the figure. The direction of $\Delta \vec{B}$ is perpendicular to the plane determined by ΔL and r (the plane out of the page). In the case shown, the right-hand rule tells us that $\Delta \vec{B}$ is out of the page.

When r is in line with ΔL, then $\theta = 0$ and thus $\Delta B = 0$. This means that the field due to a straight wire at a point on the line of the wire is zero.

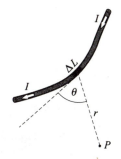

Figure 5-7

Induced EMF and Magnetic Flux

Magnetic Effects of Matter

Most materials have only a very slight effect on a steady magnetic field, and that effect is best described in terms of an experiment.

Suppose that a very long solenoid or a toroid is located in a vacuum. With a fixed current in the coil, the magnetic field at a certain point inside the solenoid or toroid is B_0, where the subscript '0' stands for vacuum. If now the solenoid or toroid core is filled with a material, the field at that point will be changed to a new value B. We define:

Relative permeability of the material = $k_M = \dfrac{B}{B_o}$

Permeability of the material = $\mu = k_M \mu_o$

Recall that μ_0 is the permeability of free space, $\mu_0 = 4\pi \times 10^{-7}$ T • m/A.

Diamagnetic materials have values for k_M slightly below unity (0.999 984 for solid lead, for example). They slightly decrease the value of B in the solenoid or toroid.

Paramagnetic materials have values for k_M slightly larger than unity (1.000 021 for solid aluminum, for example). They slightly increase the value of B in the solenoid or toroid.

Ferromagnetic materials, such as iron and its alloys, have k_M values of about 50 or larger. They greatly increase the value of B in the toroid or solenoid.

Magnetic Field Lines

A magnetic field may be represented pictorially by lines, to which $\vec{B}$ is everywhere tangential. These magnetic field lines are constructed in such a way that the number of lines piercing a unit area perpendicular to them is proportional to the local value of B.

Magnetic Flux

The **magnetic flux** (Φ_M) through an area A is defined to be the product of B_1 and A, where B_1 is the component of $\vec{B}$ perpendicular to the surface of area A:

$$\Phi_M = B_1 A = BA \cos \theta$$

where θ is the angle between the direction of the magnetic field and the perpendicular to the area. The flux is expressed in *webers* (Wb).

Induced EMF

An **induced emf** exists in a loop of wire whenever there is a change in the magnetic flux through the area surrounded by the loop. The induced emf exists only during the time that the flux through the area is changing.

Faraday's Law for Induced EMF

Suppose that a coil with N loops is subject to a changing magnetic flux through the coil. If a change in flux $\Delta\Phi_M$ occurs in a time Δt, then the average emf induced between the two terminals of the coil is given by

$$\mathcal{E} = -N\frac{\Delta\Phi_M}{\Delta t}$$

The emf $\mathcal{E}$ is measured in volts if $\Delta\Phi/\Delta t$ is in Wb/s. The minus sign indicates that the induced emf opposes the change which produces it, as stated generally in **Lenz's Law**.

Lenz's Law

An induced emf always has such a direction as to oppose the change in magnetic flux that produced it. For example, if the flux is increasing through a coil, the current produced by the induced emf will generate a flux that tends to cancel the increasing flux. Or, if the flux is decreasing through the coil, that current will produce a flux that tends to restore the decreasing flux. Lenz's Law is a consequence of Conservation of Energy. If this were not the case, the induced currents would enhance the flux change that caused them to begin with and the process would build endlessly.

Motional EMF

When a conductor moves through a magnetic field so as to cut field lines, an induced emf will exist in it, in accordance with Faraday's law. In this case,

$$|\mathcal{E}| = \frac{\Delta\Phi_M}{\Delta t}$$

The symbol $|\mathcal{E}|$ means that we are concerned here only with the magnitude of the average induced emf; its direction will be considered below.

The induced emf in a straight conductor of length L moving with velocity $\vec{v}$ perpendicular to a field $\vec{B}$ is given by

$$|\mathscr{E}| = BLv$$

where $\vec{B}$, $\vec{v}$, and the wire must be mutually perpendicular.

In this case, Lenz's Law still tells us that the induced emf opposes the process. But now the opposition is produced by way of the force exerted by the magnetic field on the induced current in the conductor. The current direction must be such that the force opposes the motion of the conductor. Knowing the current direction, we also know the direction of $\mathscr{E}$.

Electric Generators and Motors

Electric Generators

Electric generators are machines that convert mechanical energy into electrical energy. A simple generator that produces an ac voltage is shown in Figure 5-8.

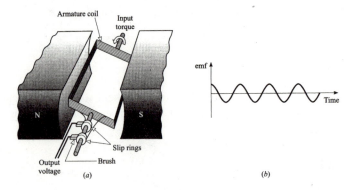

Figure 5-8

An external energy source (such as a diesel motor or a steam turbine) turns the armature coil in a magnetic field $\vec{B}$. The wires of the coil cut the field lines, and an emf

$$\mathscr{E} = 2\pi \text{NABf} \cos 2\pi \text{ft}$$

is induced between the terminals of the coil. In this relation, N is the number of loops (each of area A) on the coil, and f is the frequency of its rotation. Figure 5-8(b) shows the emf in graphical form.

As current is drawn from the generator, the wires of its coil experience a retarding force because of the interaction between current and field. Thus, the work required to rotate the coil is the source of the electrical energy supplied by the generator. For any generator,

(input mechanical energy) = (output electrical energy) +

(friction and heat losses)

Usually the losses are only a very small fraction of the input energy.

Electric Motors

Electric motors convert electrical energy into mechanical energy. A simple dc motor (i.e., one that runs on a constant voltage) is shown in Figure 5-9. The current through the armature coil interacts with the magnetic field to cause a torque

$$\tau = \text{NIAB} \sin \theta$$

on the coil, which rotates the coil and shaft. Here, θ is the angle between the field lines and the perpendicular to the plane of the coil. The split-ring commutator reverses I each time $\sin \theta$ changes sign, thereby ensuring that the torque always rotates the coil in the same sense. For such a motor,

Average torque = (constant) |NIAB|

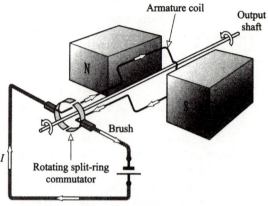

Figure 5-9

Because the rotating armature coil of the motor acts as a generator, a *back* (or *counter*) *emf* is induced in the coil. The back emf opposes the voltage source that drives the motor. Hence, the net potential difference that causes current through the armature is

Net p.d. across armature $=$ (line voltage) $-$ (back emf)

Armature current $= \dfrac{\text{(line voltage)} - \text{(back emf)}}{\text{armature resistance}}$

The mechanical power P developed within the armature of a motor is

P = (armature current)(back emf)

The useful mechanical power delivered by the motor is slightly less, due to friction, windage, and iron losses.

Inductance; R-C and R-L Time Constants

Self-Inductance

A coil can induce an emf in itself. If the current in a coil changes, the flux through the coil due to the current also changes. As a result, the changing current in a coil induces an emf in that same coil.

Because an induced emf $\mathscr{E}$ is proportional to $\Delta\Phi_M/\Delta t$ and because $\Delta\Phi_M$ is proportional to Δi, where i is the current that causes the flux,

$$\mathscr{E} = -(\text{constant})\frac{\Delta i}{\Delta t}$$

Here i is the current through the same coil in which $\mathscr{E}$ is induced. (We shall denote a time-varying current by i instead of I.) The minus sign indicates that the self-induced emf $\mathscr{E}$ is a back emf and opposes the change in current.

The proportionality constant depends upon the geometry of the coil. We represent it by L and call it the *self-inductance* of the coil. Then

$$\mathscr{E} = -L\frac{\Delta i}{\Delta t}$$

For $\mathscr{E}$ in units of V, i in units of A, and t in units of s, L is in *henries* (H).

Mutual Inductance

When the flux from one coil threads through another coil, an emf can be induced in either one by the other. The coil that contains the power source is called the *primary coil*. The other coil, in which an emf is induced by the changing current in the primary, is called the *secondary coil*. The induced secondary emf $\mathscr{E}_s$ is proportional to the time rate of change of the primary current, $\Delta i_p/\Delta t$:

$$\mathscr{E}_s = M\frac{\Delta i_p}{\Delta t}$$

where M is a constant called the *mutual inductance* of the two-coil system.

Energy Stored in an Inductor

Because of its self-induced back emf, work must be done to increase the current through an inductor from zero to I. The energy furnished to the coil in the process is stored in the coil and can be recovered as the coil's current is decreased once again to zero. If a current I is flowing in an inductor of self-inductance L, then the energy stored in the inductor is

$$\text{Stored energy} = \frac{1}{2}LI^2$$

For L in units of H and I in units of A, the energy is in J.

R-C Time Constant

Consider the R-C circuit shown in Figure 5-10(a).

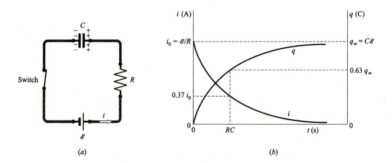

(a) (b)

Figure 5-10

The capacitor is initially uncharged. If the switch is now closed, the current i in the circuit and the charge q on the capacitor vary as shown in Figure 5-10(b). If we call the p.d. across the capacitor v_c, writing the loop rule for this circuit gives

$$-iR - v_c + \mathscr{E} = 0 \qquad \text{or} \qquad i = \frac{\mathscr{E} - v_c}{R}$$

At the first instant after the switch is closed, $v_c = 0$ and $i = \mathscr{E}/R$. As time goes on, v_c increases and i decreases. The time, in seconds, taken for the current to drop to 1/2.718 or 0.368 of its initial value is RC, which is called the *time constant of the R-C circuit.*

Also shown in Figure 5-10(b) is the variation of q, the charge on the capacitor, with time. At t = RC, q has attained 0.632 of its final value. When a charged capacitor C with initial charge q_0 is discharged through a resistor R, its discharge current follows the same curve as for charging. The charge q on the capacitor follows a curve similar to that for the discharge current. At time RC, $i = 0.368i_0$ and $q = 0.368q_0$ during discharge.

R-L Time Constant

Consider the circuit in Figure 5-11(a) with a resistor of resistance R ohms and a coil of self-inductance L henries. When the switch in the circuit is first closed, the current in the circuit rises, as shown in Figure 5-11(b). The current does not jump to its final value because the changing flux through the coil induces a back emf in the coil, which opposes the rising current. After L/R seconds, the current has risen to 0.632 of its final value i_∞. This time, t = L/R, is called the *time constant of the R-L circuit.* After a long time, the current is changing so slowly that the back emf in the inductor, $L(\Delta I/\Delta t)$, is negligible. Then $i = i_\infty = \mathscr{E}/R$.

Exponential functions are used as follows to describe the curves of Figures 5-10 and 5-11:

$i = i_0 e^{-t/RC}$ capacitor charging and discharging

$q = q_\infty \left(1 - e^{-t/RC}\right)$ capacitor charging

$q = q_\infty e^{-t/RC}$ capacitor discharging

$i = i_\infty \left(1 - e^{-t/(L/R)}\right)$ inductor current buildup

where e = 2.718 is the base of the natural logarithms.

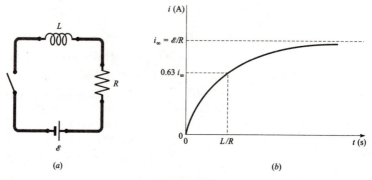

Figure 5-11

When t is equal to the time constant, the relations for a capacitor give $i = 0.368i_0$ and $q = 0.632q_\infty$ for charging, and $q = 0.368q_\infty$ for discharging. The equation for current in an inductor gives $i = 0.632i_\infty$ when t equals the time constant.

The equation for i in the capacitor circuit (as well as for q in the capacitor discharge case) has the following property:

After n time constants have passed,

$$i = i_0 (0.368)^n \text{ and } q = q_\infty (0.368)^n$$

For example, after four time constants have passed,

$$i = i_0 (0.368)^4 = 0.0183i_0$$

Alternating Current

Alternating Current

The emf generated by a rotating coil in a magnetic field has a graph similar to the one shown in Figure 5-12.

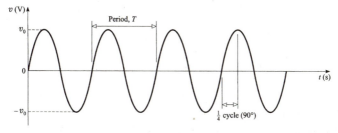

Figure 5-12

It is called an *ac voltage* because there is a reversal of polarity (i.e., the voltage changes sign); ac voltages need not be sinusoidal. If the coil rotates with a frequency of f revolutions per second, then the emf has a frequency of f in hertz (cycles per second). The instantaneous voltage v that is generated has the form

$$v = v_0 \sin \omega t = v_0 \sin 2\pi ft$$

where v_0 is the amplitude (maximum value) of the voltage in volts, $\omega = 2\pi f$ is the angular velocity in rad/s, and f is the frequency in hertz. The frequency f of the voltage is related to its period T by

$$T = \frac{1}{f}$$

where T is in seconds.

Rotating coils are not the only source of ac voltages; electronic devices for generating ac voltages are very common. Alternating voltages produce alternating currents. An alternating current produced by a typical generator has a graph much like that for the voltage shown in Figure 5-12. Its instantaneous value is i, and its amplitude is i_0. Often the current and voltage do not reach a maximum at the same time, even though they both have the same frequency.

Meters for use in ac circuits read the *effective*, or *root mean square* (rms), values of the current and voltage. These values are always positive and are related to the amplitudes of the instantaneous sinusoidal values through

$$V = V_{rms} = \frac{v_o}{\sqrt{2}} = 0.707 v_o$$

$$I = I_{rms} = \frac{i_o}{\sqrt{2}} = 0.707 i_o$$

It is customary to represent meter readings by capital letters (V, I), while instantaneous values are represented by small letters (v, i).

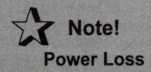

Note!

Power Loss

The thermal energy generated or power lost by an rms current I in a resistor R is given by I^2R.

Forms of Ohm's Law

Suppose that a sinusoidal current of frequency f with rms value I flows through a pure resistor R, or a pure inductor L, or a pure capacitor C. Then an ac voltmeter placed across the element in question will read an rms voltage V as follows:

Pure resistor: $V = IR$
Pure inductor: $V = IX_L$
        where $X_L = 2\pi fL$ is called the *inductive reactance*.
        Its unit is ohms when L is in henries and f is in hertz.
Pure capacitor: $V = IX_C$
        where $X_C = 1/2\pi fC$ is called the *capacitive reactance*.
        Its unit is ohms when C is in farads.

Phase

When an ac voltage is applied to a pure resistance, the voltage across the resistance and the current through it attain their maximum values at the same instant and their zero values at the same instant; the voltage and current are said to be *in-phase*.

When an ac voltage is applied to a pure inductance, the voltage across the inductance reaches its maximum value one-quarter cycle ahead of the current, i.e., when the current is zero. The back emf of the inductance causes the current through the inductance to lag behind the voltage by one-quarter cycle (or 90°), and the two are 90° *out-of-phase*.

When an ac voltage is applied to a pure capacitor, the voltage across it lags 90° behind the current flowing through it. Current must flow before the voltage across (and charge on) the capacitor can build up.

In more complicated situations involving combinations of R, L, and C, the voltage and current are usually (but not always) out-of-phase. The angle by which the voltage lags or leads the current is called the *phase angle*.

Impedance

The **impedance** (Z) of a series circuit containing resistance, inductance, and capacitance is given by

$$Z = \sqrt{R^2 + \left(X_L - X_C\right)^2}$$

with Z in ohms. If a voltage V is applied to such a series circuit, then a form of Ohm's Law relates V to the current I through it:

$$V = IZ$$

The phase angle ϕ between V and I is given by

$$\tan \phi = \frac{X_L - X_C}{R} \quad \text{or} \quad \cos \phi = \frac{R}{Z}$$

Phasors

A **phasor** is a quantity that behaves, in many regards, like a vector. Phasors are used to describe series R-L-C circuits because the above expression for the impedance can be associated with the Pythagorean theorem for a right triangle. As shown in Figure 5-13(a), Z is the hypotenuse of the right triangle, while R and (X_L - X_C) are its two legs. The angle labeled ϕ is the phase angle between the current and the voltage.

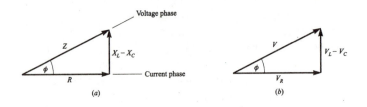

Figure 5-13

A similar relation applies to the voltages across the elements in the series circuit. As shown in Figure 5-13(b), it is

$$V^2 = V_R^2 + \left(V_L - V_C\right)^2$$

Because of the phase differences, a measurement of the voltage across a series circuit is not equal to the algebraic sum of the individual voltage readings across its elements. Instead, the above relation must be used.

Resonance

Resonance occurs in a series R-L-C circuit when $X_L = X_C$. Under this condition, Z = R is minimum, so that I is maximum for a given value of V. Equating X_L to X_C, we find for the *resonant* (or *natural*) *frequency* of the circuit

$$f_o = \frac{1}{2\pi \sqrt{LC}}$$

Power Loss in the Impedance

Suppose that an ac voltage V is impressed across an impedance of any type. It gives rise to a current I through the impedance, and the phase angle between V and I is ϕ. The **power loss in the impedance** is given by

Power loss = VI cos ϕ

The quantity cos ϕ is called the *power factor*. It is unity for a pure resistor; but it is zero for a pure inductor or capacitor (no power loss occurs in a pure inductor or capacitor).

Transformer

A **transformer** is a device to raise or lower the voltage in an ac circuit. It consists of a primary and a secondary coil wound on the same iron core. An alternating current in one coil creates a continuously changing magnetic flux through the core. This change of flux induces an alternating emf in the other coil.

The efficiency of a transformer is usually very high. Thus, we may neglect losses and write

Power in primary = power in secondary
$$V_1 I_1 = V_2 I_2$$

The voltage ratio is the ratio of the numbers of turns on the two coils; the current ratio is the inverse ratio of the numbers of turns:

$$\frac{V_1}{V_2} = \frac{N_1}{N_2} \quad \text{and} \quad \frac{I_1}{I_2} = \frac{N_2}{N_1}$$

Solved Problems

Solved Problem 5.1 The charges shown in Figure SP5-1 are stationary. Find the force on the 4 μC charge due to the other two.

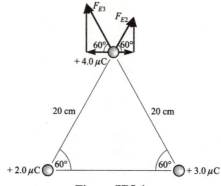

Figure SP5-1

Solution. From Coulomb's law, we have:

$$F_2 = k\frac{qq'}{r^2} = (9 \times 10^9 \text{ N m}^2/\text{C}^2)\frac{(2 \times 10^{-6} \text{ C})(4 \times 10^{-6} \text{ C})}{(0.20 \text{ m})^2} = 1.8 \text{ N}$$

$$F_2 = k\frac{qq'}{r^2} = (9 \times 10^9 \text{ N m}^2/\text{C}^2)\frac{(3 \times 10^{-6} \text{ C})(4 \times 10^{-6} \text{ C})}{(0.20 \text{ m})^2} = 2.7 \text{ N}$$

The resultant force on the 4 µC charge has components:

$$F_x = F_2 \cos 60° - F_3 \cos 60° = (1.8 - 2.7)(0.5) \text{ N} = -0.45 \text{ N}$$

$$F_y = F_2 \sin 60° + F_3 \sin 60° = (1.8 + 2.7)(0.866) \text{ N} = 3.9 \text{ N}$$

So, $F = \sqrt{F_x^2 + F_y^2} = \sqrt{(0.45)^2 + (3.9)^2} \text{ N} = 3.9 \text{ N}$

The resultant makes an angle of arctan (0.45/3.9) = 7° with the positive y-axis, that is θ = 97°.

Solved Problem 5.2 The charge shown in Figure SP5-2 is a proton (q = +e, m = 1.67 x 10⁻²⁷ kg) with speed 5 x 10⁶ m/s. It is passing through a uniform magnetic field directed out of the page; B is 30G. Describe the path followed by the proton.

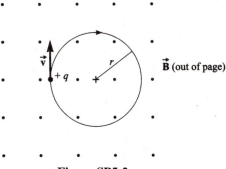

Figure SP5-2

Solution. Because the proton's velocity is perpendicular to **B**, the force on the proton is

q v B sin 90° = q v B

The force is perpendicular to **v** and so it does no work on the proton. It simply deflects the proton and causes it to follow the circular path shown, as you can verify using the right-hand rule. The force q v B is radially inward and supplies the centripetal force for the circular motion:

$$qvB = \frac{mv^2}{r} \quad \text{or} \quad r = \frac{mv}{qB} \tag{1}$$

For the given data,

$$r = \frac{(1.67 \times 10^{-27} \text{ kg})(5 \times 10^6 \text{ m/s})}{(1.67 \times 10^{-19} \text{ C})(30 \times 10^{-4} \text{ T})} = 17.4 \text{ m}$$

Observe from (1) that the momentum of the charged particle is directly proportional to the radius of its circular orbit.

Chapter 6
LIGHT AND GEOMETRICAL OPTICS

IN THIS CHAPTER:

✔ *Reflection of Light*
✔ *Refraction of Light*
✔ *Thin Lenses*
✔ *Optical Instruments*
✔ *Interference and Diffraction of Light*
✔ *Solved Problems*

Reflection of Light

Light (along with all other forms of electromagnetic radiation) is a fundamental entity, and physics is still struggling to understand it. On an observable level, light manifests two seemingly contradictory behaviors, crudely pictured via wave and particle models. Usually the amount of energy present is so large that light behaves as if it were an ideal continuous wave, a wave of interdependent electric and magnetic fields. The interaction of light with lenses, mirrors, prisms, slits, and so forth, can satisfactorily be understood via

the wave model. On the other hand, when light is emitted or absorbed by the atoms of a system, these processes occur as if the radiant energy is in the form of minute, localized, well-directed blasts; that is, as if light is a stream of particles. Fortunately, without worrying about the very nature of light, we can predict its behavior in a wide range of practical situations.

Law of Reflection

A ray is a mathematical line drawn perpendicular to the wavefronts of a lightwave. It shows the direction of propagation of electromagnetic energy. In *specular* (or *mirror*) reflection, the angle of incidence equals the angle of reflection, as shown in Figure 6-1. Furthermore, the incident ray, reflected ray, and normal to the surface all lie in the same plane, called the *plane-of-incidence*.

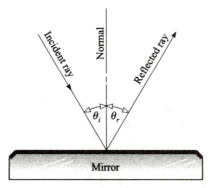

Figure 6-1

Plane Mirrors

Plane mirrors form images that are erect, of the same size as the object, and as far behind the reflecting surface as the object is in front of it. Such an image is *virtual*; i.e., the image will not appear on a screen located at the position on the image because the light does not converge there.

Spherical Mirrors

The *principal focus* of a spherical mirror, such as the ones shown in Figure 6-2, is the point F where rays parallel to and very close to the *central* or *optical axis* of the mirror are focused. This focus is real for a concave mirror and virtual for a convex mirror. It is located on the optical axis and midway between the center of curvature C and the mirror.

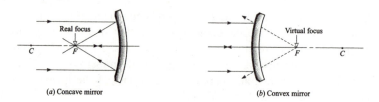

(a) Concave mirror   (b) Convex mirror

Figure 6-2

Concave mirrors form inverted real images of objects placed beyond the principal focus. If the object is between the principal focus and the mirror, the image is virtual, erect, and enlarged.

Convex mirrors produce only erect virtual images of objects placed in front of them. The images are diminished (smaller than the object) in size.

Mirror Equation

The **mirror equation** for both concave and convex spherical mirrors is

$$\frac{1}{s_o} + \frac{1}{s_i} = \frac{2}{R} = \frac{1}{f}$$

where s_o = object distance from the mirror
   s_i = image distance from the mirror
   R = radius of curvature of the mirror
   f = focal length of the mirror = R/2

In addition,

- s_o is positive when the object is in front of the mirror.
- s_i is positive when the image is real, i.e., in front of the mirror.
- s_i is negative when the image is virtual, i.e., behind the mirror.
- R and f are positive for a concave mirror and negative for a convex mirror.

The **size of the image** formed by a spherical mirror is given by

$$\text{Linear magnification} = \frac{\text{length of image}}{\text{length of object}}$$

$$= \frac{\text{image distance from mirror}}{\text{object distance from mirror}} = \left| \frac{s_i}{s_o} \right|$$

Refraction of Light

Speed of Light

The **speed of light** as ordinarily measured varies from material to material. Light (treated macroscopically) travels fastest in vacuum, where its speed is $c = 2.998 \times 10^8$ m/s. Its speed in air is $c/1.000\ 3$. In water, its speed is $c/1.33$, and in ordinary glass it is about $c/1.5$. Nonetheless, on a microscopic level, light is composed of photons and photons exist only at the speed c. The apparent slowing down in material media arises from the absorption and re-emission as the light passes from atom to atom.

Index of Refraction

The **absolute index of refraction of a material** is defined as

$$n = \frac{\text{speed of light in vacuum}}{\text{speed of light in the material}} = \frac{c}{v}$$

For any two materials, the **relative index of refraction** of material-1, with respect to material-2, is

$$\text{Relative index} = \frac{n_1}{n_2}$$

where n_1 and n_2 are the absolute refractive indices of the two materials.

Refraction

When a ray of light is transmitted obliquely through the boundary between two materials of unlike index of refraction, the ray bends. This phenomenon, called **refraction**, is shown in Figure 6-3.

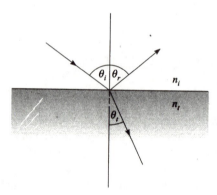

Figure 6-3

If $n_t > n_i$, the ray refracts as shown in the figure; it bends toward the normal as it enters the second material. If $n_t < n_i$, however, the ray refracts away from the normal. This would be the situation in Figure 6-3 if the direction of the ray were reversed. In either case, the incident and refracted (or transmitted) rays and the normal all lie in the same plane. The angles θ_i and θ_t in Figure 6-3 are called the *angle of incidence* and *angle of transmission* (or refraction), respectively.

Snell's Law

The way in which a ray refracts at an interface between materials with indices of refraction n_i and n_t is given by **Snell's Law**:

$$n_i \sin \theta_i = n_t \sin \theta_t$$

where θ_i and θ_t are as shown in Figure 6-3. Because this equation applies to light moving in either direction along the ray, a ray of light follows the same path when its direction is reversed.

Critical Angle for Total Internal Reflection

When light reflects off an interface where $n_i < n_t$, the process is called *external reflection*; when $n_i > n_t$, it is *internal reflection*. Suppose that a ray of light passes from a material of higher index of refraction to one of lower index, as shown in Figure 6-4.

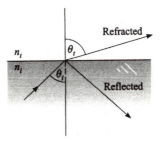

Figure 6-4

Part of the incident light is refracted and part is reflected at the interface. Because θ_t must be larger than θ_i, it is possible to make θ_i large enough so that $\theta_t = 90°$. This value for θ_i is called the **critical angle θ_c**. For θ_i larger than this, no refracted ray can exist; all the light is reflected. The condition for total internal reflection is that θ_i exceed the critical angle θ_c, where

$$n_i \sin \theta_c = n_t \sin 90° \quad \text{or} \quad \sin \theta_c = \frac{n_t}{n_i}$$

Because the sine of an angle can never be larger than unity, this relation confirms that total internal reflection can occur only if $n_i > n_t$.

Prism

A **prism** can be used to disperse light into its various colors, as shown in Figure 6-5. Because the index of refraction of a material varies with wavelength, different colors of light refract differently. In nearly all materials, red is refracted least and blue is refracted most.

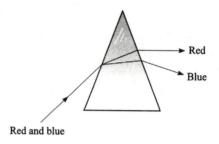

Figure 6-5

Thin Lenses

Types of Lenses

As indicated in Figure 6-6, *converging*, or *positive*, lenses are thicker at the center than at the rim and will converge a beam of parallel light to a real focus. *Diverging*, or *negative*, lenses are thinner at the center than at the rim and will diverge a beam of parallel light from a virtual focus.

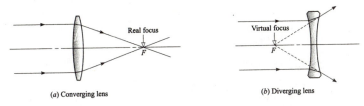

(a) Converging lens   (b) Diverging lens

Figure 6-6

The *principal focus* (or *focal point*) of a thin lens with spherical surfaces is the point F where rays parallel to and near the central or optical axis are brought to a focus; this focus is real for a converging lens and virtual for a diverging lens. The *focal length* f is the distance of the principal focus from the lens. Because each lens in Figure 6-6 can be reversed without altering the rays, two symmetric focal points exist for each lens.

The object and image relation for converging and diverging lenses is

$$\frac{1}{s_o} + \frac{1}{s_i} = \frac{1}{f}$$

where s_o is the object distance from the lens, s_i is the image distance from the lens, and f is the focal length of the lens. The lens is assumed to be thin, and the light rays *paraxial* (close to the principal axis). Then,

- s_o is positive for a real object, and negative for a virtual object.
- s_i is positive for a real image, and negative for a virtual image.
- f is positive for a converging lens, and negative for a diverging lens.

Also,

$$\text{Linear magnification} = \frac{\text{size of image}}{\text{size of object}}$$

$$= \frac{\text{image distance from lens}}{\text{object distance from lens}} = \left| \frac{s_i}{s_o} \right|$$

You Need to Know ✔

Converging lenses form inverted real images of objects located outside the principal focus. When the object is between the principal focus and the lens, the image is virtual (on the same side of the lens as the object), erect, and enlarged.

Diverging lenses produce only virtual, erect, and smaller images of real objects.

Lensmaker's Equation

$$\frac{1}{f} = (n-1)\left(\frac{1}{r_1} - \frac{1}{r_2}\right)$$

where n is the refractive index of the lens material, and r_1 and r_2 are the radii of curvature of the two lens surfaces. This equation holds for all types of thin lenses. A radius of curvature, r, is positive when its center of curvature lies to the right of the surface, and negative when its center of curvatures lies to the left of the surface.

If a lens with refractive index n_1 is immersed in a material with index n_2, then n in the lensmaker's equation is to be replaced by n_1/n_2.

Lens Power

Lens power in *diopters* (m^{-1}) is equal to 1/f, where f is the focal length expressed in meters.

Lenses in Contact

When two thin lenses having focal lengths f_1 and f_2 are in close contact, the focal length f of the combination is given by

$$\frac{1}{f} = \frac{1}{f_1} + \frac{1}{f_2}$$

For lenses in close contact, the power of the combination is equal to the sum of their individual powers.

Optical Instruments

Combination of Thin Lenses

To locate the image produced by two lenses acting in combination,

(1) Compute the position of the image produced by the first lens alone, disregarding the second lens.

(2) Then consider this image as the object for the second lens, and locate its image as produced by the second lens alone.

This latter image is the required image.

If the image formed by the first lens alone is computed to be behind the second lens, then that image is a virtual object for the second lens, and its distance from the second lens is considered negative.

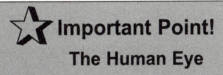

Important Point!
The Human Eye

The **human eye** uses a variable-focus lens to form an image on the retina at the rear of the eye. The *near point* of the eye, represented by d_n, is the closest distance to the eye from which an object can be viewed clearly. For the normal eye, d_n is about 25 cm. *Farsighted* persons can see distinctly only objects that are far from the eye; *nearsighted* persons can see distinctly only objects that are close to the eye.

Magnifying Glass

A **magnifying glass** is a converging lens used so that it forms an erect, enlarged, virtual image of an object placed inside its focal point. The magnification due to a magnifier with focal length f is $(d_n/f) + 1$ if the image it casts is at the near point. Alternatively, if the image is at infinity, the magnification is d_n/f.

Microscope

A **microscope** that consists of two converging lenses, an objective lens (focal length f_o) and an eyepiece lens (f_e), has

$$\text{Magnification} = \left(\frac{d_n}{f_e} + 1\right)\left(\frac{q_o}{f_o} - 1\right)$$

where q_o is the distance from the objective lens to the image it forms. Usually, q_o is close to 18 cm.

Telescope

A **telescope** that has an objective lens (or mirror) with focal length f_o and an eyepiece with focal length f_e gives a magnification $M = f_o/f_e$.

Interference and Diffraction of Light

Coherent Waves

Coherent waves are waves that have the same form, the same frequency, and a fixed phase difference (i.e., the amount by which the peaks of one wave lead or lag those of the other wave does not change with time).

The **relative phase** of two coherent waves traveling along the same line together specifies their relative positions on the line. If the crests of one wave fall on the crests of the other, the waves are *in-phase*. If the crests of one fall on the troughs of the other, the waves are 180° (or one-half wavelength) *out-of-phase*.

Interference Effects

Interference effects occur when two or more coherent waves overlap. If two coherent waves of the same amplitude are superposed, *total destructive interference* (cancellation, darkness) occurs when the waves are 180° out-of-phase. *Total constructive interference* (reinforcement, brightness) occurs when they are in-phase.

Diffraction

Diffraction refers to the deviation of light from straight-line propagation. It usually corresponds to the bending or spreading of waves around the edges of apertures and obstacles. Diffraction places a limit on the size of details that can be observed optically.

Single-Slit Diffraction

When parallel rays of light of wavelength λ are incident normally upon a slit of width D, a diffraction pattern is observed beyond the slit. Complete darkness is observed at angles $\theta_{m'}$ to the straight-through beam, where

$$m'\lambda = D \sin \theta_{m'}$$

Here, $m' = 1, 2, 3, \ldots$, is the *order number* of the diffraction dark band.

Limit of Resolution

The **limit of resolution** of two objects due to diffraction:

If two objects are viewed through an optical instrument, the diffraction patterns caused by the aperture of the instrument limit our ability to distinguish the objects from each other. For distinguishability, the angle θ subtended at the aperture by the objects must be larger than a critical value θ_{cr}, given by

$$\sin \theta_{cr} = (1.22)\frac{\lambda}{D}$$

where D is the diameter of the circular aperture.

Diffraction Grating Equation

A **diffraction grating** is a repetitive array of apertures or obstacles that alters the amplitude or phase of a wave. It usually consists of a large number of equally spaced, parallel slits or ridges; the distance between slits is the grating spacing a. When waves of wavelength λ are incident normally upon a grating with spacing a, maxima are observed beyond the grating at angles θ_m to the normal, where

$$m\lambda = a \sin \theta_m$$

Here, m = 1, 2, 3, . . ., is the *order number* of the diffracted image.

This same relation applies to the major maxima in the interference patterns of even two and three slits. In these cases, however, the maxima are not nearly so sharply defined as for a grating consisting of hundreds of slits. The pattern may become quite complex if the slits are wide enough so that the single-slit diffraction pattern from each slit shows several minima.

Diffraction of X-Rays

The **diffraction of x-rays** of wavelength λ by reflection from a crystal is described by the *Bragg equation*. Strong reflections are observed at grazing angles ϕ_m (where φ is the angle between the face of the crystal and the reflected beam) given by

$$m\lambda = 2d \sin \phi_m$$

where d is the distance between reflecting planes in the crystal, and m = 1, 2, 3, . . ., is the *order* of reflection.

Optical Path Length

In the same time that it takes a beam of light to travel a distance d in a material of index of refraction n, the beam would travel a distance nd in air or vacuum. For this reason, nd is defined as the **optical path length** of the material.

Solved Problems

Solved Problem 6.1 What is the critical angle for light passing from glass (n = 1.54) to water (n = 1.33)?

Solution.

$$n_1 \sin \theta_1 = n_2 \sin \theta_2 \quad \text{becomes} \quad n_1 \sin \theta_c = n_2 \sin 90°$$

from which

$$\sin \theta_c = \frac{n_2}{n_1} = \frac{1.33}{1.54} = 0.864 \quad \text{or} \quad \theta_c = 59.7°$$

Solved Problem 6.2 A camera gives a clear image of a distant landscape when the lens is 8 cm from the film. What adjustment is required to get a good photograph of a map placed 72 cm from the lens?

Solution. When the camera is focused for distant objects (for parallel rays), the distance between lens and film is the focal length of the lens, 8 cm. For an object 72 cm distant:

$$\frac{1}{q} = \frac{1}{f} - \frac{1}{p} = \frac{1}{8} - \frac{1}{72} \quad \text{or} \quad q = 9 \text{ cm}$$

The lens should be moved farther away from the film a distance of (9 - 8) cm = 1 cm.

Index